The

ULTIMATE

HORSE
lover

**The Best Experts' Advice for a
Happy, Healthy Horse with Stories and
Photos of Awe-Inspiring Equines**

Marty Becker, D.V.M.
Gina Spadafori
Audrey Pavia
Mikkel Becker

**Health Communications, Inc.
HCI Books, the Life Issues Publisher
Deerfield Beach, Florida**

*www.hcibooks.com
www.ultimatehcibooks.com*

We acknowledge the writers and photographers who granted us permission to use their material. A copyright credit appears on each interior photograph and credits for literary work are listed alphabetically by authors' last names. Contact information, as supplied by the photographers and writers, can be found in the back matter of this book.

Horse Sense. ©Lynn Allen. All rights reserved. Previously published in La Junta *Tribune-Democrat* and as part of *Life Out Here* (Cheraw Publishing, 2008, Cherawpublishing.com).

Shoot Your Horse: With a Camera, Of Course! ©Sarah K. Andrew. All rights reserved.

A Lifetime of Love. ©Sarah K. Andrew. All rights reserved.

On the Road: Tips for Trailering and Travel. ©Mark R. Baus, D.V.M. All rights reserved.

(*Copyright Credit continued on page 247*)

Library of Congress Cataloging-in-Publication Data

The ultimate horse lover: the best experts' advice for a happy, healthy horse with stories and photos of awe-inspiring equines / Marty Becker
. . . [et al.].
    p. cm.
    Includes index.
    ISBN-13: 978-0-7573-0752-2 (trade paper)
    ISBN-10: 0-7573-0752-3 (trade paper)
    1. Horses—United States—Anecdotes 2. Horsemen and horsewomen—United States—Anecdotes. 3. Human-animal communication—United States—Anecdotes. I. Becker, Marty, 1954-
    SF301.U48 2008
    636.1—dc22
                                      2008033960

©2008 Marty Becker, D.V.M., Gina Spadafori, Audrey Pavia, Mikkel Becker

Publisher: Health Communications, Inc.
        3201 S.W. 15th Street
        Deerfield Beach, FL 33442-8190

Cover Design: Larissa Hise Henoch
Photo: ©Jose Manuel Gelpi Diaz
Photo Editor: Justin Rotkowitz
Interior Design: Lawna Patterson Oldfield

*We dedicate this book to every horse who
lavishes gifts on a human family.*

*To the families who make sure their horses'
health and happiness are a priority.*

*To all members of the veterinary healthcare team
and everyone involved with animal treatment,
rescue, and rehabilitation.*

*To all healthcare providers who harness
the healing power of animals to improve
human health and well-being.*

*To the special love of horses as celebrated
in stories, photographs, memories,
and heartfelt emotions.*

*And finally to God for the gift of animals and the
life-affirming bond we share with them.*

Contents

Common Language

One of the Family

Unconditional Love

celebrating the Bond

Must-Know Info

Introduction

The debt we owe to horses can never be repaid except in our admiration of their beauty, their spirit, and their athleticism.

Horses have been with us for generations. They pulled our plows and our wagons, and they carried our warriors into battle. They rounded up our cattle and turned the Wild West into our home. They are so much a part of who we are that our language is rich with equine references, from "long in the tooth" to "a horse of a different color" and many more.

We no longer need horses to take our family into town or our cannons into battle, but our love for them endures. Our nation's mounted police officers, no matter how urban their beat, know that they need pause for only a minute before hearing someone ask, "May I pet your horse?"

For many that fascination, that appreciation, that love of horses extends far beyond the occasional glimpse of one or the rare encounter that allows us to pat an arched neck or feel soft whiskers brush our palm as we offer a stranger's horse a treat. For us, a life without horses—our own horses—in it is unthinkable.

We ride them, we drive them, we show them, we race them—no longer because we have to, but because we want to.

Those of us whose hearts are in this book are unabashed animal lovers. Animals are central to our lives and the work we have chosen—whether as veterinarians, writers, or photographers—and we cannot imagine living without them. We love horses, large and small, young and old, high-spirited and easygoing. Whether they live on our own acreage or in a stable we must drive to, we cannot wait to see our horses. They lift us up, physically upon their backs and emotionally with their spirits and their beauty.

We know we are not alone in the appreciation of all things equine.

Horses teach us, heal us, make us laugh, and break our hearts with their passing. We understand the benefits of equine companionship because we live with horses, love them, and care for and about them. Our lives are about helping others build better, fuller lives with their horses. The strength of the human–animal bond and the growing importance of animals in our lives are the reasons we wanted to do this book. We have cared for and about animals all of our adult lives, and we have loved them from the time we first drew breath.

The very best experts—top veterinarians, trainers, behaviorists, and other authorities—were tapped to provide valuable insights and helpful advice on all manner of equine topics, but we wanted much more: We knew horse enthusiasts had stories of equine love, loyalty, laughter, rescue, and courage, and we knew we wanted to share them as well as pictures, each worth far more than a thousand words.

From thousands of story and photo submissions we have chosen the very best—the ones we loved, the ones you'll love, too.
Celebrate the horse with us. Turn the page and enjoy.

Acknowledgments

I t takes a talented team, toiling behind the scenes, to work magic and produce a book. There are dozens of people, each with a specific niche, who brought *The Ultimate Horse Lover* from conception to creation to its place on your favorite booksellers' shelves.

Our biggest thanks go to our horses—past and present—not only for their patience while we learned how to love, nurture, and care for them, but also for simply allowing us into their world.

Thank you to everyone who submitted a story or photograph for consideration. Although we were able to use only a small portion of the thousands we received, we know that each word and picture came from a heartfelt place.

This book would not have been possible without the generosity of some of the world's top veterinarians, behaviorists, trainers, breeders, and other experts who have dedicated their careers to making life better for pets and people. You'll find all you need to know about these talented professionals following each of the "Must-Know Info" topics in which they share their expertise.

We want to acknowledge Amanda M. House, D.V.M., who served as our consultant for the essential information you'll find in this book. You can learn more about Dr. House and the pioneering work she is doing at the University of Florida in our Resources section.

We especially thank Peter Vegso, publisher of our last eight consecutive pet books, for believing in us and supporting us in myriad ways. With HCI Books there is harmony, joy, trust, flexibility, excitement, experience, professionalism, a can-do attitude, and a shared love of both pets and people. We tip our hats in sincere appreciation and respect to every member of the HCI team, whose efforts allow us to show off these books with pride!

On a more personal level, we simply cannot do what we do without the support of our family and friends.

Marty thanks his beloved wife, Teresa, son, Lex, daughter, Mikkel, and son-in-law, Pat, for their love and support. The Becker family shares Almost Heaven Ranch in northern Idaho with a menagerie of four-legged family members—dogs, cats, and horses—that are a constant source of joy. Worthy of special mention is Marty's colleague, mentor, and friend, R. K. Anderson, D.V.M., cofounder of the Delta Society, world-renowned veterinary behaviorist, inventor, and founder of abrionline.org.

Gina's love and appreciation go out to her brother Joe, who is her very best friend, her parents, Louise and Nino, her brother Pete, his wife, Sally, and their bright and talented children, Kate and Steven. Thanks to Christie Keith and Morgan Ong, friends who are really family. And, of course, to all the animals who continue to teach the lessons of love and acceptance.

Audrey couldn't have contributed to this book without the help of her greatest teachers: her horses, Milagro and Red. Their patience, love, and beauty are a constant inspiration to her. She's also grateful to her husband, Randy, for being her coach and cheerleader. And without periodic snuggles from the rest of her Norco, California, family—four cats, a dog, two rabbits, and three chickens—Audrey wouldn't have had as much fun working on this book.

Mikkel foremost thanks God for his love and blessings. Her dearly loved husband, Pat, never ceases to make her laugh and keep her life full with his on-the-edge spontaneity and fun, while her children (pugs), Willy and Bruce, keep her entertained with their wrestling and cuddling. Mikkel credits her beloved quarter horse, Chex, for helping her through the tough teen times and showing her what it's like to win blue ribbons and silver buckles. And special thanks to her family cheerleaders, who have shared her accomplishments and achievements: Marty, Teresa, Lex, Valdie, Rockey, Virginia, Joan, Pete, Mike, and Joanie, for their enduring love and support.

Marty Becker
Gina Spadafori
Audrey Pavia
Mikkel Becker

Teachers and Healers

Our Tears Mingled

By Patti Schonlau as told to Janet Perez Eckles

I was eleven years old and sick with the flu when Daddy stepped into my room. While his deep but tender voice always caressed my heart with comfort, today it made my heart beat faster. "I've got something for you, honey," he announced in a singing tone. He was holding the most beautiful saddle I'd ever seen: It was bright red and black with brilliant diamond cutouts around the edge. Its sparkle seemed to brighten my room, and I inhaled the scent of fresh leather that filled the air.

Daddy placed the saddle at the foot of my bed. Pushing aside the covers, I ran my fingers slowly across the cool, smooth seat. I looked up at him and beamed. "Do you like it?" he smiled back. He knew that something for my four-legged friend Scout would delight me more than any other present. "I guess even the flu can't keep you from enjoying your gift." He laughed and bounced the saddle on the bed, mimicking a bucking bronco. The new saddle seemed to make my flu symptoms all but disappear.

"Scout will love this!" I exclaimed.

The next day, with the saddle in my hands, I headed to the barn to see Scout. As usual, he stood in the back stall, hiding in a shadowed corner, looking scared. It was no wonder. Daddy and I had gotten him from a sale barn three months earlier. He was scrawny and scared of everything—especially men. We suspected he had been abused and neglected. Even so, there was something about him that Daddy and I couldn't resist. Once we got him home, I spent every day in the barn with Scout, stroking him, talking to him, and feeding him. As soon as I saw him, I quickened my steps.

"There you are," I murmured. I could feel the soft dirt under my feet and smell the strong odor of wet hay. I drew closer and whispered, "Hey, boy, look what I have for you." I swung the saddle up and positioned it on his back, taking a step back to observe his reaction. He held his head higher and looked from side to side with seeming pride. The colors of the saddle accented his shiny, dark-brown coat, and he seemed transformed from a skinny, shy horse to the strong, radiant equine he was meant to be.

When we spent precious moments together Scout became my warrior, my defender, and my confidant. Countless rides over familiar paths became our routine, and it seemed he grew to know me better than I knew myself. The passing years faded some of the radiance of the red and black saddle, but my relationship with Scout shone more brightly than ever. Even at seventeen, I still revealed my fears and joys only to him. No one else listened as he did.

One afternoon as Scout grazed peacefully, the sun's rays striking his coat and a soft breeze lifting his mane, my world shook violently in a whirlwind of emotion many miles away. As I sat in the examining room for a routine eye checkup, the ophthalmologist abruptly announced, "She has a retinal disease for which there is no cure." I sank in the chair, unable to breathe, the horrid news pressing like bricks into my chest.

"I'm afraid it will eventually take her sight. It's only a matter of time." He spoke as if I weren't there. On the way home, Daddy's light comments broke the silence, but my blaring fear drowned them out.

Each passing day brought dreaded evidence of my diminishing peripheral vision. The retinal condition dimmed the light of my surroundings and also dropped a veil of gloom over my soul. As my eyesight deteriorated, so did my desire to enjoy activities that had brightened my teen years. Conflicting emotions tore at my heart.

"Do you need any help picking out your clothes?" Daddy asked in a soft voice one day.

"No, I can do it myself!" I shouted back. I was angry at the world. I could only imagine the look on his face as he walked out. I threw my clothes down, flung myself onto the bed, and sobbed. Colors and shapes, vibrant and inviting before, now faded into the dark gray of my surroundings. Coordinating my clothes, a task I once performed with pleasure and ease, was now impossible.

"Any time you need to go anywhere, just let us know," my friends offered. "You know we're here for you." Their tone rang with compassion. Sure, I appreciated their support, but they couldn't know the turmoil that plagued my heart.

When they made plans to see a movie, they added, "You can go, too, if you want."

"No, that's okay. I'll just go home," I replied quickly. With tears trickling down my cheeks, I made my way across the grass, following the sounds coming from the barn. I found the stall where my loyal friend waited and hugged his muscular neck, feeling the warmth of his body. Scout stood still, listening to my sobbing whispers. He understood more than just my words. Gratefully, I stroked his face with palms wet from my tears. He seemed to cry with me: *You're not alone. I'm hurting, too.*

Scout was the one, the only one, who seemed to understand my anguish, fear, and frustration. When I cried into his neck, he nickered softly and nuzzled my shoulder with his velvet nose. I sensed his tenderness when I revealed to him my deepest pain and desperate longing. He stood by me when my world sank into a dark tunnel. *I'll be here for you. I'll be your eyes,* he seemed to say.

We still took long rides. Unlike before, I couldn't steer him around dangerous obstacles. Yet he seemed to know and he was protective of his now-sightless rider. Unable to guide him, I trusted his judgment. His steps, careful and smooth, matched his tender heart.

He proved more than capable, not only of carrying me around physical dangers, but also of easing me through emotional pitfalls. And when no one else knew how to take away the sting of living a sightless life, with each ride he gave me joy—joy that helped lighten my burdens.

With the unconditional love I felt from Scout, I slowly learned to accept the challenges of my new life. When the day came for me to leave home for college, Daddy parked the car alongside the fence so Scout could put his head through my window. As I hugged his neck, our tears mingled once again. We didn't need words. Like the beautiful saddle I had once placed on his scrawny back, he had given a shining glow of compassion and love to my broken world. Our hearts were forever braided together in a rope of unconditional love. He became my eyes, showing me the other side of a dark world. And when I was unable to express my pain, he read my heart, sensed my grief, and gave me the strength to face the world on my own.

Eight Belles and the Challenge of Faith

By Chaplain Ken Boehm
as told to Chaplain Ed Donnally

As the sun rose, I walked though the Churchill Downs backstretch stable gate on Derby Day and made my way though the crush of media. As the track chaplain, I was determined to maintain my tradition of praying with the owners, trainers, and stable staff of each horse entered in the "Run for the Roses."

In the glamour and grit of Thoroughbred racing, the horse is king. Sit in the track "kitchen," and you'll rarely hear a conversation not about horses. Here, you are who you rode, groomed, exercised, shod, or hot-walked. Each morning horses' temperatures are taken, feed tubs checked for leftover oats, hooves picked, stalls cleaned, tack shined, and their all-important legs expertly inspected for any sign of swelling or heat.

Each day on the track at America's twin-spired racing cathedral, several hundred horses train; straining at their bits, relishing those moments when their riders guide them to the rail, give them rein, and bow into a crouch as they accelerate to a full "breeze" of more than forty miles an hour.

That day, Derby hopes were high for Eight Belles, a strapping, gun-metal gray girl who had grown from a playful, overgrown ugly duckling into a sleek and very serious racing star. In a few hours she would attempt to become the fourth filly to win the world's famous race, and as I stood in front of Eight Belles' stall, I prayed that the Lord would bring her back safely.

Later, I watched from the grandstand's second floor overhang as Big Brown won the race. He was the winner, no doubt, but Eight Belles would not stop trying and came in second, beating eighteen of the nation's best boys. Her triumph is one of the moments those of us who love the horses will hold in our hearts forever. But the sweetness of that memory was all too brief. Seconds later, a crackling voice came over a walkie-talkie that one of the horses had gone down.

I rushed downstairs through tens of thousands in the Derby crush to the unsaddling area where I learned from Z Fortune's jockey, Robby Albarado, that the rider was fine, but that Eight Belles had a freak accident, breaking both front ankles while pulling up.

He said it was fatal. A jockey always knows.

I hurried to the backstretch area where I knew Eight Belles would be. Stunned and near tears, I stood over her lifeless body and thanked God that her rider was safe and that he allowed her to bring joy to so many who had watched her run.

My concern then turned to the people who were close to Eight Belles; her trainer, groom, exercise rider, and owners. I drove my golf cart to Eight Belles' barn, threading my way through the throng of media to her stall, the same one she had walked from earlier on her way to the paddock. In the somber stillness, I prayed with those who cared for and loved Eight Belles, and now grieved for her. We thanked God for giving her such a great heart and prayed that something good would come out of this tragedy.

The next day when I visited, the barn was enveloped in a cloud of grief. I offered a short prayer asking God to give all of the crew patience and wisdom. Caring for their other horses was a responsibility that came as a relief. The familiar routines of being around these great and giving animals let them forget, for brief moments, the tragedy of their brave strapping filly, taken mere moments after her greatest triumph. Mourning is the price every human pays for loving.

I went home that night physically, emotionally, mentally, and in some sense, spiritually drained. None of my words could bring the brave filly back or bring solace and peace to the people who loved her, but it was a chaplain's duty to make every attempt to do just that.

It is human nature to try to understand why tragedies occur, but we don't have the mind of God and I do not question his wisdom. Instead, I have faith that something good will come from the loss of Eight Belles to further protect the race horse and advance research in prevention and treatment of equine injuries and rehabilitation.

Revelations tells us that Jesus will return riding a white horse, so I know there are horses in heaven, but my memories of that huge, steel gray filly who loved to kick up her heels, play on the track, and strike a pose when someone took her photo are no less bittersweet knowing that she has been welcomed home by a loving God.

EDITORS' NOTE: *Eight Belles had a great heart and tremendous courage. Her ashes will be buried in the Kentucky Derby Museum alongside four Kentucky Derby winners, and a memorial service held there on Derby Day 2009. The Eight Belles Memorial Fund to fund studies on preventing equine injuries has been established in her honor.*

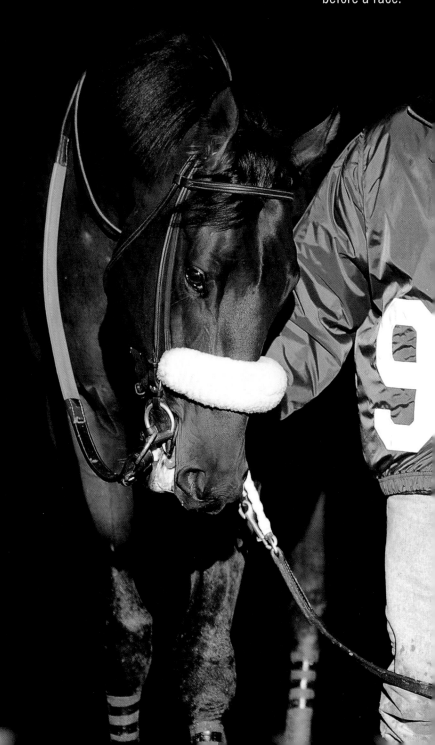

Sharing a moment
before a race.

Ponies are often used to teach children to ride because they're perfectly scaled to smaller riders.

Groom-mates. Grooming each other shows a high level of bonding and affection.

The bond with humans begins early for this young paint horse.

Snow won't stop this horse out for an early-morning run.

Like humans, horses can develop close bonds with friends.

A paint horse in a western show bridle.

The horse:
a girl's best friend.

The Here and Now
of Life with Bonnie

By Paula Ryan

When I was a little girl, I desperately wanted a horse. My whole world revolved around them. I had horse books and horse models, and there were horse drawings in the margins of all my homework. All of my recesses were spent either pretending to ride a horse or be a horse. My riding lesson was the most important hour of my week. It seemed to me that if I didn't get a horse of my own, I would die.

But I didn't get one and still I managed to survive largely because as I got older, my horse fever began to subside. My parents, completely nonhorsey people, breathed an audible sigh of relief when I started spending less time hanging around the stable and more time at the shopping mall. I still loved horses, but they were no longer the center of my world. Eventually, I stopped riding altogether.

I grew up, got married, and had a child. The years passed, and horses slipped to a back corner of my mind. I still thought they were beautiful, but I categorized them as "things I used to do" along with trick-or-treating and dress up—so much fun, but not for a grown-up. I didn't have the time or the money. Horses were not part of my adult life. Then one day I found myself longingly stroking a bronze horse sculpture as if it were a living creature. My brain finally realized that I'd been deluding myself and a giant horse-shaped piece of my heart was missing. I went straight home and started calling about riding lessons.

After the first one, I came home and told my husband, "I have to have a horse." I didn't tell him that if I didn't get one, I would die. But I think it was implied.

A year later, I was finally looking for my own horse. That's when I met Bonnie. My husband's coworker was selling her and invited me to meet her. I was looking for a gelding, preferably a Morgan, old enough to be experienced, and dark bay or black. Bonnie? Bonnie was a six-year-old paint mare, primarily white with dark markings. She'd had a few months of professional training when she was three and then was never ridden again. Any fool could see she was not a good match for me.

"Oh, come on," her owner pleaded. "Just get to know her. Bonnie's a nice horse once she figures out that you're an okay human." (Bonnie's definition of an okay human is anyone holding food. But once the treats are gone, you go sliding right back down the popularity scale.)

"Oh, come on," my husband urged. "She's a Medicine Hat paint, which makes her especially cool, and she's got such a pretty face." True. She has dark markings around both eyes, as if she's wearing heavy eyeliner, which makes her look sort of like an equine Cleopatra.

But she also was massively overweight and completely inexperienced, and she had the shortest tail I'd ever seen on a horse.

Bonnie's owner told me that the cow in the next field sometimes chewed on it. This should have told me something, but fate was already at work. *Do not buy this horse*, I told myself. *She is not what you are looking for. You are going to be sorry.*

Of course, I bought her.

I made the decision one afternoon when I was hanging out with Bonnie, just brushing her. Her owner had encouraged me to spend as much time with her as I liked in the hope that I'd fall for her. While I was brushing her, I had the sudden realization that this was a horse who would never hurt me. At the time, I was leasing a cranky, old quarter horse whose main goal in life seemed to be to injure me whenever possible, so the sense I got that Bonnie had only good intentions toward me finally won me over. Besides, Native Americans believed that Medicine Hats were magical and that you could never be killed while riding one. How on earth could I possibly turn down a magical horse with such good karma?

Bonnie turned out to be a pretty laid-back horse, very smart, and more than a little stubborn. I tried hard to be the world's most responsible horse owner and I drove everybody crazy by asking for advice constantly. One thing I just couldn't figure out was this weird thing that would happen to her occasionally. Bonnie's skin would start to ripple, as if something were crawling beneath the surface, and her breathing would seem heavier than normal. Once, I dragged the barn owner down to see it, and she shrugged. "It's just flies," she told me, rolling her eyes. "Don't be so paranoid."

Turns out I was right to be paranoid. Bonnie didn't have the world's most extreme reaction to flies. She had a genetic disorder called hyperkalemic periodic paralysis (HYPP). I learned this the hard way one evening when she experienced an attack so severe that she collapsed. She lay on the ground paralyzed, blood dripping out of her mouth from where she'd bitten her tongue. As a witness to the episode, I was nearly hysterical. I thought she was dying, and even though she recovered that night, I was afraid we might not be so lucky again.

I researched her symptoms and had the appropriate tests done. To my sorrow, Bonnie was diagnosed with HYPP. I cried for hours when my suspicions were confirmed. Suddenly, my dream of having a horse had turned into a nightmare. I was afraid all the time. When I was at the barn, I was afraid to ride Bonnie for fear she'd suddenly fall again. I watched her obsessively, looking for those telltale skin ripples. When I was away from her, I tensed every time the phone rang, worried that it could be the barn with bad news. It was a dark, sad time for me, and probably for her, too.

One morning it had all gotten to be too much for me. When no one was around to see, I rested my head on the edge of her stall and started to cry. A few seconds later, I felt her lips nuzzle my hair. I looked up into her sweet, dark eyes, and she reached forward and ever so gently touched my face with her muzzle. *Hey,* she seemed to be saying. *Why are you sad? Don't you know I'm here?* I'd always loved her, but at that moment, I realized just how much. I think I'd been trying to put some emotional distance between us in the hope that it wouldn't hurt so much if she had to leave me, but I knew now I couldn't do that.

I had a few other epiphanies, too. When I was afraid to ride Bonnie, the barn owner very kindly lent me another horse. Sid was a wonderful old gelding, and I loved him. One day I said good-bye to him and left, and when I came back two days later, he was gone. He'd suffered a severe colic and had to be put down. I was stunned. I'd been riding him because I thought my horse might die. Now he was gone, and my sick horse was still alive. It really made me think.

Not long after that, one of the other horse owners at the barn told me to stop looking at Bonnie as a victim. "She doesn't know there's anything wrong with her and she doesn't care. She's just happy being a horse, living her life." This made a huge impression on me. I realized that I had been expecting Bonnie to die at any minute instead of enjoying that she was alive. I realized I needed to love my horse now and not worry about "for how long." Slowly, I worked my way back up to riding her, and now, several years later, she's still doing great. The HYPP will never go away, and, of course, I wish she didn't have it, but we've learned to live with it.

Bonnie has taught me so many things. I've learned that sometimes in life what you think you want isn't what you really want, or maybe you just don't know enough yet to want what you really ought to have. She's taught me that sometimes you go looking for a Morgan gelding and come home with a quirky paint mare because that's how it's supposed to be. She's shown that it's best not to make assumptions about the future, but to live in the moment as much as possible. I've also learned that I can handle more than I thought I could. Bonnie has taught me never to take her for granted, not for a second. I always kiss her good-bye and tell her that I love her, just in case. And I'm never stingy with carrots.

Greenhorn No More

By Melinda Stiles

T he first time I herded cows with my neighbors, I couldn't shake the feeling that I was in a Western movie, on the back of my trusty pal, Sam. I expected to see Hoss and Little Joe Cartwright ride up to greet us any minute. I inhaled the aromatic sagebrush as the cows moved through it and relished the dust they kicked up in my face. This was not work.

Sam was a friend's horse, and I didn't know his history. I knew he was gentle with this novice and that he didn't flinch when the cows ticked off a rattlesnake or one of the cowboys shot it. The second time I herded cows, my rancher neighbor had no other help. This would be a working day. Verdell and I rode in steep sagebrush-covered hills. He was looking for cows.

I couldn't get the Ponderosa out of my mind. When Verdell spotted his cows in a valley, he rode down to get them. I was going to wait for him, but Sam had other ideas. Down the hill we went—fast. Sam may have been enjoying himself more than I was at that point. We gathered a dozen cows and headed them home. As we edged them up a hill along a fence line, Verdell asked, "You feel comfortable doing this?"

"Sure. I love being out here."

"Good, because I need to go up that way and get more cows. Just follow the fence line till you get to the road. I'll meet you at the cattle guard."

He rode off before I could plead greenhorn status.

Walk the fence line. That seemed easy enough. The cows moved along. Sam and I rode to the side of them—nothing to it.

Then one heifer stopped and tried to double back. I could have worked myself into a panic, but I didn't have time. Sam doubled back and pushed the cow back into line. And then I got it. I wouldn't have to do anything but hold on. Sam knew all we needed to know about herding cows.

We got the cows down the fence line and across the road to the cattle guard. One cow made a break from the herd. Sam took off at a run (reminding me to always hold on), got behind the cow, and drove it back. He stood close to the herd, eyeing each cow. He was in control, which was more than I could say for his rider.

Sam's perked ears told me when the rest of the herd was on its way down the road to meet us. I felt so proud to be waiting on my horse, the cows right where they should be.

"Well, how was it?" Verdell asked, as he joined Sam and our portion of the herd.

I could have waxed poetic about how I felt, but I chose instead to defer to the one on our team who was completely in charge.

"Ask Sam."

Slick

By Mike Donahue

My wife, Linda, and I met and wed in Las Vegas. We got to the city by different roads and became horse lovers by dissimilar routes as well. I'm a born and bred Westerner from the dirty-hands side of ranches and farms. I flipped off the back of my first solo ride when I was five. He was a sheepherder's horse and didn't understand that my legs were too short to keep the stirrups from hitting him in the ribs—the signal for him to run fast. Fortunately, the northern Utah snow was deep and soft, and I bounced up with a lifetime hunger for more.

Linda is an Illinois native who read *Black Beauty* thirty-five times as a girl. She has always adored horses. It's in her genes. She learned to ride while helping an uncle break the stubborn Shetland ponies he used in a carnival ride. Her equine ardor grew from an all-consuming passion to an obsessive dream. That dream became a reality in the 1990s when we bought a home in the Las Vegas desert that had corrals for two horses. It wasn't long before we filled them with Slick and Christopher and began riding in dusty gullies around our place.

May in Las Vegas is transition time. Fierce spring winds have generally come and gone and, although summer has not officially arrived, daytime temperatures are starting to remind residents that we live in the Mojave Desert. For decades, the fraternal organization of Elks have staged a massive summer Western experience called Helldorado. For the general public the celebration usually starts with a trail ride and weeks later ends with a parade and a huge five-day Professional Rodeo Cowboys Association rodeo and carnival. It's a time when locals celebrate their Western heritage and support worthy Elks causes at the same time.

In 1994, Linda and I decided to participate more fully in Helldorado by joining the trail ride. For a small fee, we could contribute to the Elks, enjoy riding our horses in a new setting, and mingle with good local people. That year the two-day trail event was held a few miles north of the city on the sloping foothills of majestic Mount Charleston, which rises to 11,918 feet. The May trail ride was to be in an area merely cool at night but comfortable by day.

I trailered Slick and my horse, Christopher, to the trailhead Friday night. Linda joined me Saturday and we excitedly got ready to ride. The area was dotted with horse trailers and small camps of participating Las Vegans. Smoke from campfires mingled with the singular aroma of horse manure. It wafted down the mountain and was filtered by jutting Joshua trees and stubby, pungent sage. It was distinct, familiar, and marvelous. Horses neighed and good friends met and laughed in camaraderie. Everywhere were porta-potties, cowboy hats, and the jingle of tack and spurs. It was the Old West come to life.

About 8 AM we mounted and joined the group threading its way through the Joshua trees and scrub brush. The sky was a heart-melting, cloudless blue. There was a light breeze. It looked like it was going to be a glorious day. Looks, however, can be deceiving. By 8:15 we were less than 300 yards from camp, and Slick was acting like a complete moron. He snorted, turned, spun, and repeatedly charged. A thoroughbred that once raced on California tracks, he began to prance and dance as though he was entering the starting gate for the biggest race of his life. Every time he made a move off the trail, he got stuck by sharp spears of Joshua leaves. It made him crazy. Linda did a marvelous job of fighting to control the big dark bay, but it wasn't enough. He was beyond control.

Suddenly, Slick gave a small buck, spun, and then reared like the Lone Ranger's horse, Silver. Unlike Silver, however, Slick did not drop back down. At the top of his rear, he just kept going backward. He was 16.2 hands and weighed about 1,200 pounds. In the blink of an eye, all that weight was falling into my wife's lap. Time slowed to an agonizing crawl. I could see everything. I knew what was about to happen, but I could do nothing to prevent it. I was helpless.

And Linda—poor Linda. She, too, knew what was happening. She was molded to the saddle. Later she told me that her mind was filled with the horrible vision of the saddle horn punching through her diaphragm. Time for her, too, was moving like frigid molasses.

I watched that marvelous dark gelding fall backward onto Linda. His heavy legs waved like thick stalks of bamboo, and he screamed. He screamed like a banshee from hell. The blood curdled in my veins, and my heart turned to lead, but I moved.

Before the brush had finished cracking, I was off Christopher and racing toward what I thought was my dead wife.

Suddenly, as fast as Slick had gone down, he rolled to his feet and began running like he was leading a throng of racers on the last turn at Santa Anita. It was as though he knew what had happened and he was running to escape the horror that had been under him. I dropped on the rocky trail beside Linda, my heart breaking. I scanned her supine body for twisted limbs, spurting blood, and bubbling guts. Instead I found myself gazing into her beautiful blue eyes. She was alive. She was alive and looking right back at me. There was no blood, no guts, no apparent broken bones.

"Medevac!" she screamed. "Medevac! Get the helicopter and get me to the hospital."

My God she's alive, I thought. "Don't move," I yelled back at her. "Don't move. Don't move." My screams were echoed by others who were dropping from their horses to rush to her side. *How in the hell can she be alive?* I thought. *And there's no blood.*

"We've already called for the chopper," one frantic woman said. "It was already on the way when this happened." It turned out that another rider's horse had also rolled on top of him. He, however, wasn't so lucky. He had stopped breathing.

We later determined that rather than coming straight down on top of Linda, Slick had made a slight roll. Instead of getting pinned to the rocks and dirt, Linda had landed on a cushy, fluffy purple sage. Slick had half landed on her right leg. She ended up sore but it wasn't bad. Nevertheless, we didn't know that at the time, and as I stood watching the helicopter fly away I wondered if I would ever see my wife again. Slick had been caught and returned to me, and I loaded him and Christopher and headed for town.

The staff at University Medical Center x-rayed Linda from the blond hair on her head to the toes on her feet to check for fractures. They couldn't have been more thorough. There were no injuries from the crash with Slick, but there turned out to be something else, something perhaps much worse than getting hurt by a nutty horse. During the comprehensive physical, a tiny shadow was spotted. It turned out to be the most virulent form of breast cancer.

We were devastated. But Linda entered the battle for her life with both hands punching and both legs kicking. It wasn't easy, but her determination paid off and she is alive today, more than thirteen years later, thanks to surgery, weeks of horrible chemotherapy, and an unbelievable will to survive.

And yes, a lot of the credit goes to a hapless bay thoroughbred with kind brown eyes named Slick. Without him, without the crash, Linda's cancer may have gone undetected until it was too late. Slick never again acted crazy, not on the trail, not in the arena. After that one incident on the slopes of Mount Charleston, Slick just kind of hunkered down to live the quiet life. We never did understand what set him off.

Slick hadn't made the grade on the California track but he was more of a hero to Linda and me than if he'd won the Kentucky Derby. His presence in our lives will never be forgotten.

# Lovim's Story

Don MacDonald Jr. as told to Arthur Montague

When I first met Lovim, the bay gelding was nearly past his prime as a trotter. His owner, Les Rickman, still entered him in races whenever he could, and Lovim's poor showings didn't disappoint Les as much as frustrate him because he knew the horse had fine potential. Unfortunately, no one wanted to drive him.

Lovim had a bad reputation among harness drivers, and I was no exception. He was what we called a toe sticker: he would stop on a dime if another horse got in front of him. He didn't do it every time, just often enough to make him a danger to his driver and every driver coming up behind. On the other hand, when Lovim got a lead, he held it. The horse was strong and stubborn and, except for his quirk, he was a competitor who never gave up. Neither did Les.

My introduction to Lovim came early in the 1982 season at the Western Fair track in London, Ontario. I was signed to drive a couple races that day and hoped to catch a couple more. Les's offer to have me drive Lovim wasn't exactly the answer to my prayer, but I did not have a lot of choices.

I was twenty-two, with enough years as a harness driver and standardbred trainer behind me to figure there wasn't a horse I couldn't handle, except maybe Lovim. But the gelding needed a race and so did I. That night I was more concerned with keeping him (and myself) out of harm's way than in winning the race. We finished far back, and I found it a chore to do so. Lovim knew what he was supposed to be doing—get ahead and stay ahead. Holding him back to keep him out of traffic wore me out.

Les was happy enough with the way I handled the horse. He even suggested I spend some time training Lovim, if only to get to know him a little better. I went to work, mostly trying to figure out how to stop him toe sticking when he got in traffic. When he trotted alone, he was clocking well. No wonder Les saw his potential. This was a horse that loved what he was doing. He just didn't like other horses ahead of him.

It turns out that Lovim had the solution all along. He just needed a while before he trusted me enough to show me.

The day finally came. We started a race from the far outside and stayed there throughout. Lovim won going away. Bingo! After that win, no matter what our starting position, I began putting Lovim on the outside as quickly as possible. He won eight straight races and was headed toward being the Western Fair meet's winningest horse.

Then late in the season, Lovim had yet another surprise for me. He was trotting on the outside and in the two spot as we turned for home when the reins slipped from my hands. Without control I was powerless, but Lovim knew what was expected of him. He breezed past the tiring leader and handily won the race.

I recovered the reins in time to jog him to the winner's circle, knowing now this horse was his own master. I was just being hauled along for the ride.

Les eventually sold Lovim, and I went on to other horses and other racetracks. Then in 1984, I became ill with what I thought was a severe cold. My timing couldn't have been worse. I'd married just the year before, and my wife was expecting a baby. My career was on the upswing, and we'd just made a down payment on a house. The illness was no cold; I had heart disease. Without a transplant, I'd be dead in a few months, perhaps weeks. I was put on a waiting list. I was twenty-four.

Family and friends rallied to sustain my spirits. The harness-racing community helped with financial support. Someone seemed always to be by my bedside, but there were times, late at night, when I was alone. I could feel my heart struggling with each beat and realized that as it deteriorated, other organs would starve and shut down. Every breath meant racking pain.

During those periods when one dose of painkiller was wearing off and the next had yet to be injected, I became lucid. Thoughts driven by pain and, yes, fear, became clear. I would sometimes be angry at not knowing if a donor heart would be located in time, and I was aware of the torment my wife was suffering. It was now November and our baby was due in December. Then for reasons I don't understand, I reached out and found an improbable new strength and confidence.

In those moments, an image of Lovim kept coming into my thoughts. He'd known what he wanted and had the will to go after it, and apart from a bad habit or two, he'd always been up for a race and always wanted to win. Lovim had struggled with injuries and carried the inevitable scars that come from years of racing. Yet I knew that if called upon, he would race through his pain. He wasn't a great horse but he became an anchor. He had kept me in the race even when I dropped the reins.

On December 13, 1984, I received a new heart. Ten days later my son was born. In May 1985, I drove a horse into the winner's circle at Western Fair. Now, nearly twenty-five years later, I'm no longer racing but I'm still going strong. However, those dark, silent nights in the hospital, illumined only by thoughts of Lovim, are not the end of his story.

By the end of January, barely a month after my surgery, I was back at the track, albeit as a spectator. Perhaps it was the second time back, maybe the third, but reading the form I saw my old friend Lovim entered in a race.

I was shocked. Here I was, well on the road to recovery, but here was Lovim, dropped down in class and trotting in a lowly $1,500 claiming race. From that level and given his age, he would have nowhere else to go. He finished out of the money.

Horses had always been a business for me. There had never been room for much sentiment. In that context, buying Lovim was plain stupid. He was old, arthritic, worn beyond his years. If he was lucky, he might be bought as a buggy horse. If he wasn't lucky—and many horses aren't—he'd go to a slaughterhouse.

But forget business. Even though I was broke, I cajoled Les Rickman into partnering with me to buy Lovim. He loaned me the money for my share. Lovim was important to him, too; he didn't need much persuading.

We went down to the barns that night to strike a deal. I could see Lovim was tired. He had done his best in the race but his best was no longer enough. His age was showing, but I could see the same resolute spirit in his eyes. If called to race again he would, and he would do the absolute best he could.

Les and I never raced Lovim again. More than any horse I'd ever worked with, the gelding deserved retirement from the track. We donated him to a stable that provided riding opportunities for disabled children and adults. Lovim immediately took to his new role and soon became a favorite, especially with the children. For him, the beat went on, as it has for me.

Worth a Queen's Ransom

By *Theresa Peluso*

I had been told (by adults) that the horses were magical. Some made a point to emphasize that wasn't a figure of speech, but a fact.

I had also been told to spray myself with bug repellent, which I hadn't done, so I swatted mosquitoes and wiped sweat from my face while I waited for our riders to mount. As a new volunteer at a therapeutic riding center, I silently vowed next time to listen to all the advice of my fellow, more seasoned side walkers.

Our group entered the shady canopy of the woods and we felt the temperature drop a few degrees on this brutally hot August day in Florida. At a small clearing a few yards from the trailhead, the instructor, Andrea, asked the handlers to bring the horses to a halt.

"Okay, let's get ready for our ride," Andrea said. "Hannah, what do you have in store for today's adventure?"

Hannah was the oldest of the three students riding that afternoon. An exceptionally bright ten-year-old challenged by cerebral palsy, she delighted in Andrea's weekly assignment of creating adventures for the group. Hannah loved to read, enjoyed school, and had a vivid imagination. Each weekly adventure was well prepared and researched, and no one but Hannah knew what it would be until she handed out the assignments.

"Andrea, you are Inspector Clouseau and you will meet me in London," Hannah explained. "Theresa, you are my new assistant, which is a very important job."

"And, Hannah, who are you?" I asked.

"I'm Nancy Drew and I'm an amateur detective who has become famous for solving mysteries," she replied.

I smiled, remembering that at Hannah's age I devoured every Nancy Drew book as soon as it was available at our local library. I was surprised and pleased to know that a new generation was hooked.

Hannah, in the persona of Nancy Drew, continued. "The Queen called. We're urgently needed in London. Three of her prized jumpers have been kidnapped while on their way to the Longines Royal International Horse Show. Theresa, book our tickets on the Concorde and be sure Clouseau knows we're coming. We will need his help on this one."

The other two riders in today's class were girls a few years younger than Hannah. Diagnosed with autism spectrum disorders, neither Carney nor Dawn communicated verbally, although Carney was prone to mouth words without making a sound. As a result, and because she was the natural leader of the group, Hannah always led the trio on the trails and was the rider who gave the "walk on" command that our therapeutic riding horses are trained to move forward on. Today, things would be different.

"Carney, you will lead us today," Hannah said. "You and Dawn are the McGregor brothers and you are the ones who have kidnapped the Queen's horses. You will have a head start while Theresa and I meet up with Inspector Clouseau."

"Carney . . . Dawn! How cool is that!" Andrea exclaimed. "Carney will lead today, and you are the *bad* guys!" Andrea's enthusiasm spread among the nine volunteers, but Carney and Dawn exhibited no sign of engaging in our adventure.

"Okay Carney, let's get these horses moving. The McGregor brothers need a huge head start on Nancy Drew and Inspector Clouseau. What do we say to move forward?" Andrea prodded.

"Come on, Carney, let's get going. What do we have to say to get Fred to move?" Hannah chimed in. "You know what it is. You can do it."

At the sound of Hannah's voice, Carney looked up and smiled. She and Hannah shared a special bond and it was obvious Carney wanted to please her.

"I'll help you, Carney. Say 'walk on' with me," Hannah continued to encourage. Carney's mouth moved, forming the words, and this time instead of silence came a whispered "waaak on."

"Carney, *yes*! That's very good," Andrea enthused. "Can you say it just a little louder? I don't think Fred heard you."

Andrea whispered to Fred's handler to cue him to move forward at the sound of Carney's command. "Come on. Tell Fred what you want to do, Carney."

Stronger and more clearly this time, Carney said "walk on," and just like magic, Fred moved forward down the trail followed by the other McGregor brother. A mile-wide smile broke out on

Carney's face, and her riding team cheered while Nancy Drew and her assistant waited for the always-late Clouseau.

"Ah, Mademoiselle Drew, so nice to see you again," Clouseau said with a flourish as he kissed Nancy's hand in greeting. "I understand you are searching for some missing horses, no?"

"Yes, Clouseau. And the kidnappers left a ransom note for the Queen," Nancy explained. "They are demanding $20 million by five o'clock today or the Queen will never see her horses again. We have to ride hard to get to the meeting place on time, so let's go."

Being the new addition to the team, I wasn't aware that Carney rarely verbalized, let alone so forcefully, or showed much emotion. Hannah was clearly excited for Carney and she begged Andrea to let her trot her mount, TK, so they could catch up to the other riders.

Students like Hannah, who have little or no strength or movement in their legs, rely on the horse's handler to control the pace and side walkers to keep them balanced in the saddle. While the program's goal is for students to achieve as much independence in riding as they are safely capable of doing, Hannah had never trotted before.

Andrea acquiesced to Hannah's pleading. "Okay, Hannah. Let's try it. We'll trot from here to where the trail bends to the left to see how it feels. And if you're in trouble, what do you shout?"

"RED ALERT!" Hannah replied enthusiastically.

TK's handler gave the command and he easily moved into a slow trot. Her other side walker and I supported Hannah, keeping her in the center of the horse's broad back as we jogged on each side of him. "We're trotting, Andrea! Look, we're trotting!" Hannah squealed in delight.

Before we knew it, we were at the bend, and TK's handler slowed him with a "whoa." TK came to a smooth halt with Hannah in balance and sitting tall.

"Let's do it again. *Please. Please.* I was okay. I didn't lose my center. Please Andrea can I do it again?" Hannah pleaded.

"Ah, Mademoiselle Drew, I think I see some signs of horses ahead," Andrea said, slipping into the character of Clouseau. "Look, there. A pile of poop! And (sniff, sniff) yes, it is fresh poop. There are horses ahead!"

"Shhh Clouseau, they'll hear you," warned Nancy. "I'll bet they are right around this bend. We must be careful not to scare them away. Let me go ahead and see," our intrepid detective offered.

Sure enough, just around the bend, Nancy Drew found the McGregor brothers waiting.

"We are here to pay the Queen's ransom," Nancy announced to the kidnappers.

Fred's handler moved Carney closer to TK and Hannah. Reaching into her shirt pocket with difficulty due to her limited dexterity, Hannah pulled out slips of Monopoly money and handed them to Andrea.

"Ah, let's see if the Queen's ransom should be paid. Bring me her horses," Inspector Clouseau ordered. Andrea mimed a careful inspection of three invisible horses, and as Clouseau she declared, "The Queen's horses are unhurt, and you McGregors are now rich." With that, she took Carney's hand and turned it palm up. Slowly she counted out the Monopoly cash and dramatically placed it in Carney's open hand. "Five. Ten. Fifteen. Twenty million dollars! Now, be off with you McGregors, before the Queen's men come and arrest you."

Carney looked down at the brightly colored paper and closed her hand around it and Fred's reins. Smiling, she looked at Hannah and Andrea and mouthed the words, but no sound came out. When Fred didn't move, she sat straighter in the saddle, took a deep breath, and commanded "walk on." This time, Fred moved forward without the benefit of a secret cue from the handler. Carney beamed and another cheer went up. Fred whinnied his approval.

Andrea hung back, clearly moved by it all. Casually, Hannah said, "We have to tell Carney's daddy we heard her tell Fred to 'walk on.'" Addressing me in particular she continued, "You know, Carney doesn't talk." As the importance of what I just witnessed sank in, Andrea regained her composure and rejoined our team.

"Mademoiselle Drew, it is getting late and we must hurry or I will miss my plane. Does this horse not move any faster?" The twinkle in Andrea's eyes gave no hint that she had been blinking back tears just a moment before. We steadied Hannah in her saddle, and once more TK kicked into a slow trot. This time we maintained the pace until we caught up with the rest of the group waiting at the trailhead, ready to go back to the barn.

"Carney. Dawn. Wasn't that fun, today?" Andrea exclaimed. "Wasn't that a great adventure Hannah cooked up for us? Such a shame we have to head back now."

Andrea approached Carney, who was still clutching the

Monopoly money, and held out her own hand, palm up. Carney looked at Andrea's outstretched hand and back to hers holding the colorful pieces of paper.

Thoughtfully, Carney took the first bill and placed it in Andrea's open hand. Clearly, as if it happened all the time, six-year-old Carney said "Five." Everyone remained quiet, not willing to break the spell, as Fred turned his head to look at his tiny rider.

Deliberately, Carney placed the second bill carefully in Andrea's hand, and said "Ten." Then the next, "Fifteen." And, as she laid the last piece of paper in Andrea's palm, Carney smiled and said, "Twenty."

It was over 90 degrees in the shade of those trees, but every person had goose bumps as well as tears in their eyes. Fred broke the spell with another whinny, waiting.

"Walk on!" Carney commanded unprompted.

"Walk on!" Hannah shouted.

The group moved forward. Quiet and thoughtful during the short walk back to the barn, all of us knew we had just shared an important day in the lives of two little girls. One who trotted her horse for the first time, not once, but twice, and the other who broke through a veil of silence to verbally communicate with confidence and assurance. There was no doubt that I had just witnessed magic. I couldn't wait for next week's adventure.

An Oldenburg mare used in an equine therapy program.

Given the option, how many of us would rather kiss a horse than a human?

Peek-a-boo.

Although most horses today are domesticated, the herd mentality still plays a major role in equine behavior.

Stall guards such as this one are used to give a horse a room with a view.

And they're off. The winner gets the carrots!

Rearing is usually a
playtime stunt to show off
or to let out some energy.

Tacked in western and gentle snaffle, this horse awaits his turn in the arena.

A Lesson in Respect

By *Kelly Mount*

As a child in Huntington Beach, California, I was blessed with an athletic little copper-colored mustang who perfectly matched my petite frame. Keno and I didn't think we were too small for anything and we dared anyone to tell us that we were.

Keno was my partner and he was as fiery and daring as I was. He could run as fast as the wind and jump the moon. He was a lot of horse, but we respected each other. One sunny afternoon, he reminded me to always show that respect.

I had tacked up Keno for a ride. My plan was to school him in the arena on the flat and then take him on a relaxing trail ride. Unfortunately, I'd had a tough day at school, and my mood was not very good. I was fifteen and full of raging hormones.

I grumbled as I mounted, no doubt with a frown on my face. We headed for the rail on a loose rein.

I soon found myself irritated at Keno because he was not reading my mind and going where I wanted him to go. I sharply closed my left leg on him. He accommodated me. *Good thing for you*, I thought angrily. *I'm not in the mood for any nonsense.* I asked him for a leg yield, but he did not respond quickly enough. I muttered as I jerked the reins to punish him.

As our ride continued, Keno failed to react quickly enough several more times. I smacked him and jerked on the reins in retaliation. With each incident, I grew madder and madder. Then suddenly Keno stopped dead in his tracks. He raised his head, his ears angled back toward me. I became irate. *How dare he!* I was going to teach him a lesson.

I lifted my legs up and out, as far from his sides as I could. I had plenty of time to think about what I was going to do as my little horse stood rock still. *Boy, are you going to get it,* I thought as I raised my knees high—something refined hunt-seat riders never do—and then slammed my legs into his barrel with all the strength I had.

Much to my surprise, my usually sensitive horse did not move a muscle. Normally, I had to be careful how much leg I used on him because he was very forward. But this time, despite my huge kick, he just stood in place, frozen like a statue.

I sat there in disbelief. Then Keno slowly tilted his head to the left and looked back at me as if to say, *What is wrong with you today?*

I was stunned at how perceptive he was. Keno's wisdom and self-respect cut right through my angry mood.

I started laughing and then crying. I leaned down and hugged his neck, sobbing while I apologized profusely for treating him so badly. He didn't deserve to have me take out my life's frustrations on him.

That day, Keno's uncharacteristic action shone light on my immaturity. I thought I was past throwing tantrums on horseback and fancied myself a very mature and talented rider. I suddenly realized I wasn't there yet and I was humbled.

During the time I had him, Keno helped me grow as a horse-woman and a person. That day, he reminded me that I should always treat horses—and myself—with respect.

A True Gentleman

By Melissa Rice

I recently met up again with a venerable old gentleman, some-one I've known for about thirteen years. He loves children. While they chatter and dance around him, he stands with a stately grace, listening and watching with his dark eyes. Like a doting grandparent, he gives lots of horsey rides, tolerating overeager thumps in the ribs from tiny riders.

In his case, horsey rides are to be expected. Macs Rockin' Rio, also known as Rocky, is a twenty-six-year-old American quarter horse. Animal lovers often assign human characteristics to pets. But scientists scoff. After all, they are dumb animals. How can they possibly think like we do?

But with certain animals, you have to wonder.

Rocky started out as a hunting horse, carrying elk hunters to shoot big game. Along the way, he learned to negotiate trail obstacles. That takes a certain combination of qualities in a horse: a steady disposition, a willingness to work in harmony with his rider, an awareness of where an obstacle is, and where and when to place his feet.

Rocky was the first horse my daughter rode. I have a photo of her at about two years of age, her feet dangling along his flanks. I remember that day clearly: Sydney clutching the saddle horn in one hand and the reins in the other while my sister led the gray gelding over logs set on the ground.

Along the way, he shared his talents with another set of riders, a group of special-needs children. Physically or cognitively challenged—sometimes both—these children all found safe harbor on Rocky's broad back.

He isn't a placid, stupid horse. On brisk days, I've watched him cavort like a Lipizzan stallion, kicking and rearing. He is also an escape artist. He figured out how to open the latch on his stall with his near-prehensile lips, and when we learned to chain his stall shut, he simply decided to let out his next-door neighbor instead.

But put a small child or someone with Down syndrome on his back, and somehow he seemed to know. Put an able-bodied adult in the saddle, and he'd test them. But children were always safe.

Once at a show, Sydney took a tumble off his back. While other horses might have spooked at a rider landing nearly under their feet, Rocky stood like a statue. And though his young riders may occasionally forget their trail pattern in a show, Rocky gets them through each obstacle, walking carefully over a bridge, stepping high over uneven logs, easing sideways up to a gate, backing through cones.

As time passed, my daughter needed a more challenging mount. Rocky was getting older, too, and needed a less-strenuous schedule.

Recently, he was given to a friend who needed someone steady and calm for her young niece. The old soldier was put back into service. His tiny rider, like so many before, dotes on him, giving him warm baths, finding him special treats, brushing his nearly white coat to a brilliant sheen.

I watched him perform again, carrying the tiny sprout on his broad back. After the show, glowing from earning ribbons in her classes, she beamed as she hugged the aging horse around the neck.

I could just about swear that the old boy smiled.

First Impressions

By Angelina Wilson

My first horse was a winged chestnut stallion with a white blaze and a right hind sock. His name was Sugarfoot, and together we explored the hills and valleys of West Virginia.

At least that was how an eight-year-old, horse-crazy girl envisioned him in her imagination.

I'd been born to a nonhorsey family living inside the city limits of a small town, so my encounters with real horses were limited—unlike my imagination.

The first time I ever had a chance to ride a real horse was at a trail-riding stable while on vacation. We didn't gallop through the woods or fly over any lakes as I'd imagined doing with Sugarfoot. Instead we walked around and around a small, fenced-in arena at the end of a lead rope.

But that was enough. I knew that real live flesh-and-blood horses were in my life to stay. Somehow, I'd make sure of that.

I jumped at any opportunity to be around a horse. Whenever my family went on vacation, I pestered my parents to take me to the nearest riding stable so I could go trail riding. Each summer, I attended a weeklong camp sponsored by my church. Activities ranged from crafts to sports, but I lived for the horsemanship classes. And when someone gave the local veterinarian a premature foal to include in her petting zoo adjacent to the clinic, I wasted no time asking the veterinarian if I could brush the baby while my mom went grocery shopping once a week at the store across the road.

But my dream of owning a horse had to wait until after college.

As soon as I had my degree in hand and a few extra dollars in my pocket, I began searching for a horse to call my own.

I enlisted the help of the riding instructor from whom I'd periodically taken lessons during college, and we combed the various listings of horses for sale.

None seemed right.

They were either too green for a beginner, too Western for an English rider, too pricey for someone with limited finances, or they just had too many problems—physical and mental.

The more horses we crossed off our list of possibilities, the more one stood out.

Murphy.

He was a 15.2-hand, gray thoroughbred gelding that my riding instructor had purchased from an equestrian college to use as a lesson horse. I'd ridden him a few times. We never really clicked, but neither were we mortal enemies.

He fit the description of the type of horse I wanted. He had been a school horse and had proven himself safe for a beginner. Yet he had enough advanced training so I could continue to learn from him for years to come. His forward style was ideal for an English rider. He was physically and more or less mentally sound. And his price tag was within my budget.

My riding instructor had half-heartedly considered selling him in the past, but the more we talked, the more obvious it became to both of us. Murphy would make a good first horse for me.

Within a couple weeks of moving him to a boarding stable closer to me, I realized he wasn't the eager-to-please, people-loving horse I had dreamed of owning.

He could sense a beginner a mile away and he knew every trick in the school-horse book.

I began questioning my decision to buy Murphy. His experience was perfect for me, but our personalities clashed.

I was convinced his single goal in life was to frustrate me. I knew one day I'd find a secret scorecard stashed somewhere in his stall. On it he would have kept track of how many times in one day he had exasperated me.

Perhaps he kept his tally in the back of that school-horse book of tricks he also had hidden somewhere—I don't know. But I was certain he had marked at least two of its chapters—the one detailing the best ways to be obnoxious and the one about the art of deliberate spooking, because those were his two favorite tricks.

He would plod along at the walk only to explode forward when I asked him to trot. That would inevitably pitch me onto his neck. As soon as I'd lose my balance, he'd pop his nose into the air and hollow his back, all the while picking up speed. That would unnerve me and I would tense every muscle in my arms, back, and legs to try to keep from getting bounced out of the saddle. That, in turn, would lead to what I called the Murphy gait. It felt like a combination of an animated, high-stepping trot in the front and an awkward, uncollected canter in the back. It was extremely uncomfortable to ride.

His favorite spook zone was near a large maple tree that grew alongside the fence at the far end of the arena. Every time we approached that tree, he would tense up. Then I would tense up. It continued to escalate until—whoosh—he'd pivot 90 degrees and begin dancing sideways. The first couple times, he successfully spun out from underneath me. After that, I managed to hang on, but the jolt would still pitch me onto his neck and ensure that I'd be even more anxious the next time we approached the spook zone.

Whenever Murphy would explode forward at the trot or prepare to spook at the maple tree during a riding lesson, my instructor would yell, "Relax! Breathe! It's no big deal!"

"Yeah, right," I would mutter. "How can I relax and act like it's no big deal when I'm being shaken like a margarita!"

The concept seemed completely insane.

Yet when my instructor rode Murphy, he seemed to enjoy showing off what he knew. Sometimes when he would trot past me I was sure I heard him snickering, *Naah-naah, naah-naah, naah-naah! You can't get me to do this.*

How could one horse have two completely different personalities? How could Murphy act like an idiot when I rode him, yet look like a Third Level dressage horse when my instructor rode him?

Maybe my instructor was right.

I decided that no matter what Murphy did, I would just go with the flow, try to relax, breathe, and act like it was no big deal. It wasn't easy, but as I began to change my mind-set, something magical happened. Little by little, day by day, week by week, Murphy and I went from working against each other to actually working together.

He quit doing the Murphy gait. He quit sticking his nose in the air and hollowing his back. He quit exploding into the trot from a walk.

He didn't quit spooking, but his spooks became more and more manageable. Eventually, I began to notice that he gave warning about ten strides ahead of the place where he planned to spook. I learned to ride him through it, and he spooked fewer and fewer times.

Nowadays, I can hop on Murphy bareback, with just a couple lead ropes attached to his halter, and canter over a series of low fences. If someone had told me when I bought him that one day I'd be able to do that, I would've laughed.

Murphy definitely wasn't what I'd imagined my first horse would be like. I'd envisioned a cooperative mount with whom I could gallop over the hills—a horse like Sugarfoot. Instead, I got a horse who gave me a boot-camp-style education in riding.

Occasionally, I have wondered what kind of rider I'd be if I'd had a more amicable and forgiving mount for my first horse, one who would have covered up my mistakes instead of exposing and amplifying them. I probably would have gotten more enjoyment from riding early on, but such a horse also could have given me a false sense of confidence in my riding ability.

Murphy, it turns out, was the perfect first horse for me after all. He taught me the riding skills and gave me the confidence I needed to take on my second horse, a thoroughbred gelding named Chrome.

Chrome looks and acts a lot like the Sugarfoot I once imagined: chestnut, white blaze, white hind sock, and he loves to fly . . . just not with wings. Yet without the thorough grounding in horsemanship that Murphy gave me, I would have been far less prepared to take flight.

Common Language

The Ghost Horses
of Shasta Farm

By *Gina Spadafori*

W hen I was in high school, my church group built a haunted house in an old barn that sat in the middle of small pastures next to a classic rambling California ranch house. Both structures were relics of a grander time, before the land surrounding them had been swallowed up by developers and paved over to build homes and stores that had long since succumbed to suburban blight.

The box stalls we used to set up our Halloween tableaus all had neglected brass nameplates on them. Shasta Playboy is the only one I remember now, but there were others, and everywhere there was the odor of what once had been, the faint smell of horse sweat and sweet hay. Near the pasture was a graveyard. Our youth-group leader thought it would set the tone for our haunted house and had tried to get the old woman who owned the place to let us set up something there, too. She wouldn't hear of it. "Stay in the barn," she said, "and leave the stable office door closed."

I did neither.

Ever the horse-crazy teen, I wanted to know everything about this long-empty barn, so the morning of our final performance,

I peeked behind the door marked "Stable Office" and caught a whiff of worn leather and musty papers. In the dim light I could see faded photographs of show jumpers and polo ponies, but afraid of being discovered, I soon retreated.

That night I slipped away from the rest of the group. With a flashlight in hand, I felt like Nancy Drew as I stumbled out to the pasture in the dark. Sure enough, some of the names on the graves matched the ones on the stalls and on the pictures in the stable office. More curious than ever, I crept back into the barn, and while the haunted house was being dismantled, I opened the stable office door and closed it quietly behind me.

In the flashlight's beam, I could see a row of dust-covered English saddles along the wall, some riding crops and bats in what looked like an umbrella stand, and bridles hanging neatly from hooks. A pair of tiny, well-worn muck boots stood in the corner, ancient mud still clinging to the soles. The photos I'd seen earlier, row after row after row, their glass dusty and in some cases cracked, all showed the same woman rider. Was she the old woman in the house? According to the picture nearest me, her name was Leone Hart (Mrs. F. B. Hart.)

I knew that name. The F. B. Hart Company had long sold semis and farm equipment in California's Central Valley, the location of the most productive and profitable farmland in the world. It was the ideal place for such a business.

Still, I had no idea at the time how much influence Leone Hart—and her ghost horses—would have on my life.

It was several years before I found myself in that barn again.

Though I'd left adolescence, my passion for horses never

diminished. As an adult, I would have loved to have found a way to make a living that included them, but as so often happens, practicality got the better of me. I ended up in the newspaper business, working for the *Sacramento Bee*. When an article on local history was being researched, I volunteered to find out Mrs. Hart's story. Like many a writer, I am shy on my own but fearless on assignment. I found someone who would share Mrs. Hart's unlisted number and I called.

"Why on earth would you want to talk to me?" she said. I thought her Texas accent only added to her mystery. "I'm too old to ride, and my horses are all as dead as both my husbands. You sound like a nice young lady, but there's nothing out here but me and a couple of old dogs."

And then she invited me for tea.

I finished the assignment but couldn't stop visiting. We were the oddest of friends—or maybe not. She wanted to talk, and I wanted to listen. She had lived as she rode, fast, fearless, and always to achieve a goal, and her stories could have filled dozens of books. More than anything, I wanted to live a life like hers— a life of horses—and she was happy to hand me the blueprint.

Leone wasn't born in the saddle, but it wasn't long before she was introduced to one. She came from Texas oil money, her father a self-made millionaire. Her brothers were cavalry officers; one was killed in World War I. She idolized her father but rarely mentioned her mother. I was never sure she had one beyond birth.

She was more tomboy than debutante, and her father sent her to Smith College in hopes of taming her headstrong nature. It didn't much help. In a Jazz Age show of rebellion, the young

Leone was playing polo in Argentina when she met a tractor salesman who'd just landed a big dealership in California. He promised her all the horses she could ride and a tractor trailer to haul them.

By the time F. B. Hart built her that barn and got her that tractor trailer, Leone was the best female polo player in the world. At that time, polo was spectacle, a game for the rich and glamorous. Leone spent a lot of her time in Hollywood, where the stars paraded in stylish jodhpurs and a few became quite good on a horse. "Will Rogers," she said, "now that man could ride."

Her best friend was fellow polo player Louise Tracy—Mrs. Spencer Tracy—and Leone snarled when I asked her about her friend's marriage. "It would have been fine, except for that woman," she said, referring to actress Katharine Hepburn. Then she softened. At least Mr. Tracy kept Mrs. Tracy well stocked with good polo ponies while he was engaged in Hollywood's worst-kept secret. Maybe it wasn't so bad a trade-off after all, she shrugged.

But it wasn't the Hollywood gossip I came to hear. I wanted to know about the horses, and she obliged, her stories moving forward decade by decade as I kept visiting. In them she grew from a horse-obsessed young girl to a wealthy matron, from a polo player to a show jumper to a breeder of racehorses. All her stories were of horses, and I couldn't have been happier. I heard all about Charles Howard long before *Seabiscuit* became a bestseller; she knew him well and his friend Bing Crosby, too. We flipped through cracked scrapbooks and dug through old files in the stable office. Even the feed bills fascinated me. After we exhausted

the stories of the stable office, we sat at her kitchen table, looking out over an empty pasture where the ghosts of thoroughbred
broodmares nursed their foals. We never visited the horse graveyard, though. That was too painful for Leone.

In my own life I was realizing the lessons of Leone and her
ghost horses, and I was learning to follow my heart. I knew I loved
both writing and animals, and soon I was combining my two pas-
sions: I was writing about animals.

My friendship with Leone lasted six years, nearly until the day
she died, a year or two before she turned ninety. ("A lady never
tells her age," she told me, so I never knew for sure.) On one of
the last afternoons we spent together, she gave me a photograph
I'd long admired of her with her favorite horse, Shasta Playboy—
the horse whose nameplate I'd first come across in the barn. The
picture always fascinated me, for in it I saw that as much as she
may have loved her husband, may have enjoyed her friends and
her glamorous, adventurous life, it was always about the horses.
She loved them as she loved nothing else, with tenderness,
fierceness, and pride.

The two of them—Leone Hart (Mrs. F. B. Hart) and her
favorite polo pony—have watched over me and nearly every word
I've written since, their picture hanging on the wall of every office
where I've had a keyboard for almost thirty years.

The horses who defined her life were ghosts to me, as purely
imaginative as the frights of the haunted house where I first met
their spirits. But even now when I look at that photo I can hear
her young voice, and I can smell the smooth leather of the reins
she holds in her elegantly gloved hand and the lusty aroma of

the stallion beside her. I can feel, more than anything, her passion and her love.

I have never forgotten the lessons of her ghost horses and I have always tried to follow her lead.

Strange how sometimes just opening a door can change your life.

This photo, circa 1930, transports you back
in time to life on Shasta Farm.

The Romance of the Red Stud

By Karen Bumgarner

T he first time I laid eyes on the magnificent red stud I was simply in awe. His copper-colored coat glistened in the sun as he trotted with his mares, his head turned toward us. I knew he was thinking that my mare, Hollie, was very pretty. And she was quite impressed with him, staring with her big doe eyes, her little bay ears pricked forward. He stopped with his small band for a moment to study us. Then we watched him turn and gallop over the hilltop. Not a nicker was heard. We stood in awed silence when he left.

That was an exhilarating day for Hollie and me. But it wasn't the last of the red stud. I soon found out that when allowed to explore, my little bay Arabian mare, Rushcreek Hollie, could track that stud. She was usually quite successful at it. Her talent allowed us to watch and photograph "Red" and his mares for the next three years.

On days when I planned to let her explore, we'd leave the trailer and I'd say to her, "Okay, you're the guide today. Where are we going?" She'd stand and look all around, sniff the air, and head out. We'd trot along, and she'd see a stud pile; stallions make large piles of manure to mark their territory. Most were given only a casual sniff. But occasionally Hollie would linger and give a pile her full attention as if she knew the horse who'd left it. Once she found the right sign, it wouldn't be long before she located the herd. I believe Hollie loved to watch Red as much as I did. Her gaze would lock on him and her eyes would follow him everywhere. When it was time to leave she'd often throw her head and snort as if to say *I'm not done yet!* But never would she nicker.

Two springs ago, several herds were slow to leave the lower-elevation flatlands, where the temperature was warm and the grass abundant. Normally, as soon as the weather warms, the horses head to the higher elevations. But on one of these fine days we were given a special treat: the red stud had a new foal in the herd.

Red stood protectively in front of his band of mares and the new arrival. He held his blazed chestnut face high, his bold eyes watching me warily. Then he flipped his head and gave a loud snort like a whistle. He circled his mares and whistled again, and they started to trot away. But they were curious. After only a few steps, they all stopped and faced me. The mare with the new foal stayed to the back. The stud once again advanced to the front of his band. A solid bay mare who had been barren for two years stood next to him.

I had never seen him this close. He was totally impressive, this horse untouched by man. His blond mane was long, tangled, and full of burrs and dreadlocks. Though a brush had never touched his coat, he shone like a new copper penny. There were several scars on his glistening hide, no doubt war wounds from fights with other stallions. He was very stout and muscular. I guessed him to be roughly ten years old. Red circled his mares again and snorted. It ended now as it had before: they stopped and studied me as I studied them.

The bay mare was always with Red, and now there was the chestnut blaze-faced mare who had birthed the foal. Three weeks earlier when I had watched the herd, this mare had not yet given birth. Another chestnut mare who was pregnant likely would foal in a couple weeks.

Hollie and I watched for a time and then left the wild ones to graze in the spring sunshine. Later that day, toward the end of our ride, we looped through their neighborhood and could see them napping.

A week later when we rode, the herds had moved into the high country. We could often spot the different bands from a distance. Interestingly, the bay stallion had mostly bays in his herd, the pinto stallion had three pintos and one solid chestnut, and the red stud had chestnuts like himself with the exception of the bay mare.

Each spring we watch the herds and see who has foals and who doesn't. I always take photos and compare them to previous years to determine which horses have switched bands and whether the young bachelors have managed to get girlfriends.

Hollie and I haven't seen Red and his herd since last summer's roundup. There is a young bay stallion with a couple mares, but Hollie isn't interested. She watches them, but her attention quickly wanes as she glances around, wondering where Red might be. It isn't the same without his presence. We aren't sure where in the hills he's hiding, or even if he's still out there, watching us from afar. But we are ever on the lookout for our favorite Owyhee wild horse.

Tricky Communication

By Cary Davis

I am often drawn to horses with people personalities. Paul's Pertty (named for his stunning looks), a 16-hand, bay quarter horse gelding with a narrow white blaze, was added to my horse family as a dressage prospect. His thoroughbred ancestry is evident in his leggy yet solid athletic build and his big, floating movement. While I felt his dignified, classy manner would work well in the show ring, I didn't anticipate many comical moments with him.

My horses are separated and stalled for their meals and then turned out in their paddock several hours later. One evening I walked out to find that Paul had been playing with the halter hanging outside his stall. I greeted him with, "Hey buddy, are you trying to tell me that you're ready to go out?" He surprised me by immediately walking over to me, putting his head over the stall door, and reaching for the halter. With the crownpiece in his mouth, he moved his head up and down, shaking the halter as if he wanted to open the buckle and make my job easier. He might as well have been saying, *What took you so long? Hurry up and get me out of here.*

I stood there smiling, watching my usually aloof horse act silly while making his answer clear. "So you're ready to go back out?" I asked. With his big, kind eyes focused on me, he released the halter and began working his lips back and forth until he had the lead line in his mouth. At that point, he flipped the end of it toward me. No one could have missed what he was saying with his antics. I laughed and told him how smart he was as I returned the halter and lead line to their hook, then tossed a rope over his neck and led him to his paddock.

The next evening, eager to see if my gifted horse would repeat his performance, I walked up to the stall door and asked if he was ready to go outside. He stepped up to greet me and put his head over the stall door, but this time he grabbed the neck rope that I had used the night before. With the center of it in his mouth, he carefully worked his way down to the knot on the end. Then he took hold of it and swung his head to one side in an attempt to throw the rope over his neck. He missed and rolled his eyes in disgust but didn't give up. He tossed it again, this time getting closer to his goal but still missing by several inches. After the third unsuccessful attempt, he tossed the end of the rope at me with a look that said, *Hey! Isn't this supposed to be your job?*

Since learning that my horse can make his wishes known, I always solicit his feedback. When I ask if he is ready to go out, and he moves to the corner of his stall and stands looking away from me, I'll ask, "Do you want to stay in tonight?" Backing further into the corner is his way of providing an affirmative answer. When he tugs on his stable blanket hanging near his stall and even tries to put his head through the neck opening, I understand that he would prefer to stay in his stall dressed in his all-weather attire.

Of course, looking for clues to better understand what my horse wants can work against me at times. If I'm in a hurry and would rather give the boys hay instead of putting them in their stalls for their individualized meals, Paul will stand at the paddock gate and toss his head up and down while whinnying and staring at me as if to say, *Hey! I'm waiting like a perfect gentleman. How can you leave me out here?*

Although I no longer can skip certain steps at feeding time, learning to listen to my horse in a different way has enhanced the bond between us and added to the entertainment value of doing chores.

The Holy Instant

By Pauline Peterson

A wonderful couple, Milt and Virginia Strand, heads the family that takes care of my horses on a farm where Arabians have been raised for generations. Their place is near heavenly wooded trails close by a river, and the barn is in a valley that feels holy to me every time I drive to it. Milt is getting older—he's somewhere in his seventies—and thanks to an old horse-related injury, he decided to take in more boarders. I feel privileged to be one of them.

I came to this boarding facility with my mare and her first foal, Kelsey, a pure Morgan who is chestnut, not black like her dam and sire. Soon Milt was bragging that if I bred my mare to his black Arabian for sure I would get a black foal. He brought up the subject every time he saw me and we would get into teasing arguments. I thought I could hold my own with this guy, but alas, I bred not once, but twice, to his black Arab stud, and "shur nuff," I got black both times.

My Morgan mare, Kayla, had been in a box stall for many days, preparing to foal. She was overdue to have her fourth foal and had started dripping her first milk; in other words, she was waxing.

I think she enjoyed making me wait, as this was the longest that she'd gone past her due date.

Meanwhile, the Strand family had company visiting from California and these folks very much wanted to see a foal being born. I had bragged that my mare would grace them with this event, as all of her other foals had been born in the evening, and I had been present. I assured them that they would not go back to California without seeing this wonderful feat of nature, courtesy of my accommodating mare. If I had been listening more intently, I would have heard God laughing

On about the tenth night following Kayla's due date, I came to the barn around my usual time of 8:30 to watch her foal. (Ha!) I broke a carrot in half as I approached her stall and fed one piece to her and the other to the mare in the next stall. Delilah also was overdue. She was one of Milt's mares and expecting her second foal. Dear Delilah took her piece of carrot in her mouth and immediately swung her rear end around to show me the little foot inside the birth sack that was sticking out underneath her raised tail.

I ran as fast as I could out of the barn and up to the house, opened the door, and yelled, "Get your camera, Delilah's foaling!" Then I ran back to the barn. Delilah was now lying in her stall, pushing with the contractions.

We moved Kayla out of her stall temporarily so the visitors could take better photos. Milt didn't need to exert himself to get down to the barn for something that was old hat to him, and since their sons weren't home, Virginia asked me to go in and tear open the birth sack to make sure the foal was breathing. Mares usually don't need any help giving birth, but these horses are the Strand family's business and are very important.

As soon as I saw the nose emerge, I pinched the birth sack and watched the pink amniotic fluid flow from it. The foal took its first breath and blinked repeatedly, trying to focus on my face. With one more contraction, and me helping by simultaneously pulling on its front legs, the newborn was completely clear of the mare. I pulled the sack off its little body and began lifting its hind leg to see if it was a boy or a girl. Suddenly, Delilah got up. Not wanting to upset her, I quickly got out of her stall.

The visitors were snapping pictures when Milt's son Jon arrived. He entered Delilah's stall and checked on the mare and foal. "It's a stud colt," he pronounced. "Everything looks good." The same couldn't be said for Jon, who looked exhausted after talking to people the whole weekend while promoting his horses at a local expo.

He turned to me and asked, "Are you going to be here for a while?"

"Sure, I'll be here most of the night watching Kayla," I answered.

"Could you make sure he nurses well?"

"Of course, I'll keep an eye on the foal," I replied, feeling honored to be asked to help.

Jon left, and the rest of us watched the delightful antics of a newborn foal attempting to stand and figure out how to get his body to work. Baby horses instinctively try to get up very soon after birth. A dam's milk faucet can't be reached from the ground, and newborns start out hungry. As they nurse, you can watch their little bodies expand by the minute. There is a very noticeable difference especially in the first hour, and the visitors were capturing this with their camera. They got tons of snapshots, and the colt was moving fairly well, lying down and getting back up again.

Finally, I was left alone in the barn. Delilah had been waxing for a long time and her milk bags were very full and tight. She must have been uncomfortable, even to the point of pain, because she would not stand still and she did not nudge her foal toward the teat. Consequently, the newborn hadn't gotten a good long drink, and for almost two and a half hours I worked to get him hooked on.

I expressed milk from Delilah's udder with my hands and let the foal suck the sticky, bluish-white liquid from my fingers. I'm sure he thought I was his mother. It was only after much work and some sweating on my part that I could get his dam to stand still so I could maneuver her baby into position and he could get a good grip on that faucet.

It was wonderful to watch him finally nurse on his own. I could hear him sucking loudly and I could see him swallowing rhythmically. When he had his fill, he lay down content while his dam watched over him.

By 1:30 in the morning, Little Stud Muffin, as I had named him, had nursed several times on his own. The night was as perfect a spring night as you could possibly imagine. All the doors in the barn were open and the humid spring air wafted through, mixing with the aroma of fresh hay. Perfectly contented horses munched quietly or snored (I'm not kidding). Only two lights were on: one in each of the mares' stalls.

I decided to take Kayla out. I clipped a lead rope to her halter, and she followed me eagerly because she knew there was new grass to eat. We walked away from the barn a bit, and I stopped. She immediately put her head down and happily munched grass as I held the lead rope. A gentle breeze blew and I looked up at the stars—so many were visible this far from any city. I wondered when the next full moon would appear and listened to the horses munching grass in the pasture just across the road. My Kelsey was in that herd, and I spoke softly to them. I got a low nicker in response to my voice.

The box stalls in the barn were full at night. Some horses stayed out all the time. There were probably thirty horses in the barn and maybe forty in different pastures around the farm. I remember feeling incredible peace at that moment and thinking how grateful I was to be there.

All of a sudden, Kayla jerked her head up. Then, at the same moment, she and all the other horses whinnied. It gave me goose bumps.

"My goodness, you're going to wake up the whole valley!" I scolded as I quickly led her back into the barn. Just as we rounded the corner inside, I heard Little Stud Muffin give his best and biggest whinny, and again all the other horses on the place trumpeted in response.

Now I understood. The horses had accepted me as one of them. My eyes filled with tears as Little Stud Muffin announced once again to the world, "I'm here!" and every horse in that valley answered back in unison, "Welcome!" I'll never forget that night and the thrill of being witness to that moment. It felt holy and I felt blessed.

The Smell of Cocoa

By Diane Wilson

A slightly sour smell, like that of an old sweater worn weeks on end, assaulted my nostrils as I entered the Maple View Retirement Community. I'd just come from a glorious ride on my horse on a sparkling autumn afternoon, so the hushed and airless atmosphere struck me doubly hard. This was life at a crawl, life without horses.

As I hurried my daughter to Mrs. Gilbert's room (she read to the woman for thirty minutes a week as part of her middle-school community-service project), I couldn't help glancing into rooms. Some were spare and tidy, others overflowed with keepsakes. One in particular, though, brought me to a halt. On the center of one wall hung a tinted photograph of a smiling woman on a chocolate-brown horse, wind fingering mane and curls, a postcard-perfect snow-capped mountain as backdrop. Intriguing.

It had been my habit to return to the lobby and thumb through a magazine until my daughter was finished, but when I passed the room with the horse photograph again, I noticed a woman sitting motionless on her couch. Curious, I knocked.

"Hello? Mrs. Weatherford?" That was the name printed in block letters on the door's plaque.

She startled before feigning a bright welcome. "Oh, hello. I'm glad you came."

I introduced myself as I entered and, pointing to the photo, said, "I couldn't help admiring your horse. Is that you in the saddle?" To my chagrin I heard myself adopting that slow, loud voice I so despised in the caregivers.

Mrs. Weatherford shot me a steely glare. "That's Cocoa. Best horse I ever owned."

"Where was the photo taken?" The scenery hinted at Colorado or maybe Wyoming.

She glanced toward the wall but her assurance faltered. "I don't exactly recall. It was a long time ago."

"Looks like you were having a good ride." The smiling woman in the photo appeared much bigger than the one shrunken on this couch. I guess that's what a horse did for you. The younger woman wore a tomato-red shirt with white pearl snaps, a Western hat pushed back to frame waves of curly auburn hair, and—something out of the movies—scalloped white chaps adorned with enormous silver conchos. She sat confidently, grinning with the thrill of being on such a fine horse.

And Cocoa was fine. Sunlight glinted off his muscled shoulder and sleek hip as he gazed, ears pricked, into the distance. His profile was too Roman-nosed for my taste, but he had a large eye shaded by a heavy forelock that enhanced his regal bearing. A mountain wind wrapped his tail around his hocks, and I smiled, recalling my own recent breezy ride. "What kind of bit is that?"

I asked, moving closer to admire the silverwork on the shank.

Mrs. Weatherford's chin lifted just a little, defiant. "I can't see well enough to tell you. My eyes are degenerated. I can't hardly see Cocoa anymore." She laced her fingers in her lap and seemed to study them. "He sure took good care of me though."

Betting this would be a lot better than some outdated, dog-eared magazine, I plopped myself into the padded rocking chair. "Tell me about him."

Mrs. Weatherford smiled slyly and leaned forward. "What's your horse's name?"

"Sammi," I replied. "But how did you know I have a horse?"

"Sweet feed." She sat back, triumphant. "I smell molasses."

Maybe her eyes weren't as sharp as they used to be but her nose had lost nothing. And she was right. I'd fed Sammi a handful of oat hay mixed with molasses just before driving to school to pick up my daughter.

"Hand-feeding makes horses nippy," she stated. "I never allowed it with mine."

"How many horses did you have?" And that slid open a door of happy horse talk that made the thirty minutes fly.

The next week and most of the ones that followed, I headed straight for Mrs. Weatherford's room as soon as I dropped off my daughter. Eleanor was Mrs. Weatherford's first name, though I felt uncomfortable calling her that. It seemed too familiar. Besides, with her second husband she'd owned a working cattle ranch—an operation of several thousand acres and several dozen hands—and petite though she was, she still managed an air of unquestionable authority. We talked about everything:

children, husbands, cooking, travel. But invariably the topic returned to horses.

She seemed as eager to listen to stories of my mare as I was to hear about her ranch horses: Cougar, the perpetually green-broke buckskin her foreman favored; Comanche, the ewe-necked roan her husband rode; Cookie and Calypso, the children's ponies; and, of course, her beloved Cocoa. Their adventures together held me spellbound, and on more than one occasion it was my daughter who was impatiently waiting in the lobby.

One day, clutching an old snapshot of a pigtailed me at my first horse show, I was shaken to find Mrs. Weatherford's room empty. The bed was neatly made, the brown-edged tendrils of her potted ivy still trailed over the windowsill. Even her spicy perfume, the one that reminded me of Christmas candles, lingered. But she was nowhere in sight.

"Mrs. Weatherford's in the hospital," said the youthful attendant who hesitated at the doorway.

"Is she all right?" My body tensed for the response.

"She fell yesterday, banged her face up pretty bad, and broke a wrist. I think she's coming back tomorrow."

I nodded and, soberly pondering how aging bodies doom horse lovers, returned to the lobby.

The next afternoon I drove to Maple View with a container of fragrant paperwhites. Spring was on the way and I wanted to share it with her.

With some apprehension I tiptoed into Mrs. Weatherford's room. I found her propped on pillows, her face a horrible splatter of purples and greens. A padded bandage covered one eye and her splinted forearm rested across her stomach.

"Mrs. Weatherford?"

"Yes?" Her voice quavered. Did she not recognize me?

"Hi, it's me. I brought you some flowers."

"That's nice." Flat, polite. No spark of the opinionated horse-woman I'd come to know. I cleared a space on her nightstand.

"You've been cleaning your saddle," she said dully, without so much as a glance at the flowers I set down.

I plopped into the rocker. "You're right."

"Neat's-foot oil." She managed to waggle a finger. "That's the secret. Paint it on thick."

We fell into a halting discussion of saddle care though I did more of the talking. Something had changed. It was as if she'd been thrown from a horse and this time wasn't getting back on. Conversation lagged and when she dozed, I quietly rose and headed for the door.

"I'm moving." The announcement stopped me. "My son wants me closer to his family. They're in Chico so I'm moving up there come Sunday."

"Sunday! That's awfully soon."

"I know," she sighed.

"I'll be back tomorrow," I promised. "You rest."

As I passed through Maple View's electronic doors I gratefully sucked in the wind-washed air. It never failed to stir in me an itch to ride. Opening the door to my truck bathed me in more smells—warmed leather, hay dust, oil, mushy apples—and gave me an idea.

The minute I got home I cleaned out an old grooming kit and began stocking it with every familiar horse scent I could capture.

Into it went a small tin of saddle soap, a stick of fly repellent, a fragrant sample of hair polish, a half-used container of pungent wound dressing, and of course, a plastic bag filled with oat hay mixed with molasses. For good measure, I added a hoof pick and a small brush. Finally, I dug out an old bridle that had made its way to the bottom of my trunk. The crown was cracked in two places and the snaffle bit pocked with rust, but I gave both a good cleaning, coaxing the leather into pliability and breathing in its wonderful aroma.

When I saw Mrs. Weatherford the next day she was already directing the packing of her things. "I hope you have room for this," I said, setting the grooming kit on her bed.

She craned her neck. "What have you got there?"

"I know you're worried about your eyes," I said, "that you won't be able to see Cocoa much longer. But you have so many great memories of him that I thought these things might keep them fresh." I opened the container of wound dressing and held it under her nose.

She grinned. "When Cocoa got himself tangled in the barbed wire after the July picnic."

I snapped open the bag of oat hay and molasses, and she sniffed.

"Molasses!" she exclaimed. She was looking brighter by the minute. Leaning in conspiratorially, she said, "I never told you, but every Sunday morning when our foreman wasn't around I made Cocoa a warm bran mash drizzled with the stuff. He gobbled it like pie."

And then I put the bridle in her lap. With her good hand she fingered the reins. Emotions flickered across her face: hope chasing happiness chasing hunger.

"You told me that Cocoa always wanted to be ridden, that all you had to do was jingle the bit and he'd come galloping to the gate. Well, I know he's not around to take care of you anymore, and maybe you'll never climb on a horse again, but it seems like you should have a bit to jingle. You know, just in case."

The smile she gave me blossomed with gritty spirit. She took hold of my hand and squeezed, and in her grip I felt the kindred fire of another horsewoman. There would be many horses in our lives, only a few as special as Cocoa or my own Sammi, but there would always be the memories of those perfect rides and, in merely picking up reins, the anticipation of the next one.

Rope Trick

By Vanessa Wright

T he barn manager approached me, clutching Pegasus's lead
rope. Her mouth was open, her eyes were glazed, her
weathered face slack with the stunned disbelief of an audience
assistant at a magic show.

I glanced at my watch. It was two hours before the horses'
evening feed. "Oh no," I sighed. "Not again."

Both friends and strangers have suggested that the phrase
"hungry as a horse" was coined to describe my gelding, Pegasus.
He has eaten half a round bale in one continuous chew, mowed
an acre of pasture to golf-turf manicured perfection in a single
morning, and gobbled a summer camp's entire picnic spread
before the children finished singing the camp's opening song. He
even taught himself how to drink through a straw, enabling him
to pad innocently around clinics and shows, slurping the tea,
juice, or soda out of every inattentive rider's thermos.

At other barns this astonishing ability to make food disappear earned him nicknames like Pigasus and Pegasaurus. But
Pegasus, however sated, was not satisfied. Tired of waiting or
hunting for meals, he turned himself from a passive customer

and sometimes-crook into a legendary conjurer. That was why at this barn they called him Pegacadabra, in honor of his incredible attempts to make food appear.

Like many fledgling magicians, he opened his act with a shell game. After bolting his morning hay, Pegasus eyed the horses in the other pastures. If they were still eating, he pranced to the fence and whinnied petulantly, punctuating each offended cry with a strike of his hoof against the gate. Where, he demanded, was his breakfast?

The barn manager, a veteran horsekeeper, was not fooled. Ignoring his clangs and bangs and trumpeting, she merely gazed at his bulging stomach and laughed at him as she stumped by, busy with the real work of her daily chores.

With a snort of frustration, Pegasus gave up the ruse. Soon enough, though, he hit upon a new trick.

"He hasn't gotten out again, has he?" I said.

The barn manager shook her head. It was her practice to lead the horses out in the morning and feed them their breakfast and lunch in the pasture, then bring them in at sundown and give them their supper and later their nighttime snack. Being so frequently fed, most of the horses gave little thought to their next meal. But not Pegasus. After vacuuming up his lunch, he quickly calculated that he would eat again only when he was back in his stall. By his reckoning then, all that stood between him and an early supper was the pasture gate.

Clearly, it was time for a little sleight of hoof.

Wedging his muzzle between the fence posts, Pegasus methodically nipped and jiggled the rope that tied the gate shut. With one final jerk of his teeth, he slipped the knot loose, and with one sweeping flourish of his foreleg, he flung the gate open.

Acres of glittering green freedom rolled away in every direction. Pegasus broke into a triumphant gallop, but his ever-lengthening thoroughbred strides whipped up only the dust and gravel of the narrow track that led to the barn. In moments, he hurtled into the main building and with a great bound that would have made the property fence, the overpass, and perhaps even the four-lane highway beyond it simply disappear, he leapt into his stall and plunged his nose into the hayrack.

It was empty. The horses' evening feed wouldn't be doled out for several more hours.

Pegasus wasn't fazed. He pirouetted smoothly, arched his head and neck into the aisle, and lifted himself into a round, rigid halt, as if an invisible barrier blocked the open door. One by one, he fixed each of the wide-eyed students and staff with a hypnotic gaze, willing them to recognize that here he was, politely and properly in his stall and, thus, they should hurry over and feed him.

To his great disappointment, the first person to reach him was the barn manager, who had brought a lead rope to take him back to the pasture. And when she deposited him inside, his disappointment plunged to despair. She had fortified the gate with a sturdy chain and the fence with an electric wire. Pegasus would not be giving any encores.

For the next few weeks, my great gray thoroughbred moped, plodding desultorily beside the barn manager as she led him in and out, nibbling listlessly at the lead rope she tied around the post.

Then late one afternoon, a student noticed him leaning his chin on the pasture gate, studying the staff as they led in the lesson horses, the barn manager following with the hay cart to deliver the evening feed. Thoughtfully, he swallowed the last wisps of his lunchtime alfalfa, slid his lips over to the knotted lead, and slowly, meditatively, began to untangle it. No doubt, he was plotting one last performance.

The barn manager's mouth opened and closed a few times soundlessly. She tugged gently at the rope in her hands, as if coaxing the words out of her daze. Finally, she spoke.

"He threw it to me," she said softly.

"Threw what?" I replied. "Not the lead rope?"

She nodded. "He untied it, picked it up in his teeth, and threw it to me as I walked by. I would have hung it up again, but when I tried, he whickered at me and rapped his hoof against the gate. I almost thought—I almost believed—that I was supposed to bring him in and had forgotten." She grinned suddenly. "Of course. He knows he gets his supper only if someone brings him into the barn. I bet he thinks that with a little hocus-pocus he can turn the clock ahead."

Pegasus's captivating performance quickly became known as his rope trick. As soon as he had polished off the last leaf of his lunchtime hay, he would plant himself beside the gate, unfasten his lead rope from the post, and wait. Each time a person passed, he would pick up the rope in his teeth and toss it, eyes hopeful, ears pricked. If the poor mark didn't catch on fast enough, he would whinny piteously and tap the edge of one hoof meaningfully against the bottom spar.

Years have passed since those enchanted young days, but Pegasus's rope trick has lost none of its charm. Every so often, I arrive at the barn and find him already inside, having beguiled someone into bringing him in early and giving him a few extra flakes of hay. As he munches the stems, he nickers from deep in his chest, a contented chuckle under which I almost think—I almost believe—I can hear him say *Pegacadabra!*

one of the family

Shy Boy: The Horse That Came in from the Wild

By *Monty Roberts*

O nce I had gained some recognition from the general public for my work, I began to receive various requests from the media. One of these was from the British Broadcasting Corporation (BBC) in London, asking for suggestions on making a program that would explain my concepts to a wide audience, not just horsepeople.

I recalled a time early in my career when I'd gone into the wilderness in the high ranges of Nevada and performed a Join-Up with Buster, a wild mustang. When I'd ridden him back to the ranch, the cowboys thought that I had found a mustang that had already been ridden. They didn't believe what I'd done. It still rankled. I had been so full of pride and excitement that day, and no one had believed me.

I suggested to the BBC that I could try to do the same thing. I would perform a Join-Up in the wild, and the cameras would be there to record the event. The BBC loved the idea and set about making the arrangements. Robert Miller, D.V.M., a veterinarian and renowned animal behaviorist, was hired to act as a referee of sorts. He would verify the legitimacy of the mustang and the procedures and ensure the horse received proper care. He would also be available for any veterinary needs that might arise.

Our first step was to adopt a wild mustang from the Bureau of Land Management, the federal agency that controls wild horses on public lands in the United States. I called this horse Shy Boy. I was careful to have no contact with him after the adoption so he would remain completely wild. The BBC also appointed an independent observer, a woman who represented the Santa Barbara County Wild Life Protective Agency. She selected a neutral, well-fenced pasture site for Shy Boy.

There I was, forty years after my experience with Buster, again in the high desert with only a wild mustang—no rope, no fences —and a film crew. Their presence gave the proceedings a different feel, for sure, but there would be no disputing what happened this time. Every moment would be recorded in living color.

Shy Boy joined-up with me in exactly twenty-four hours, as I had predicted to the BBC several months earlier in London. Here was a wild horse who chose to be with me rather than flee into the thousands of acres of wilderness that beckoned in every direction. I had a halter and surcingle on him in thirty-six hours. Each step was accomplished within a few hours of the schedule I'd set. Within seventy-two hours, I had a rider on Shy Boy's back, and he was following our saddle horses at a canter. Independent observers had verified every step. Join-Up between man and horse worked, even in the wild.

The documentary was shown around the world over the next three or so years. There are still skeptics who don't believe what I did. Psychologists could describe the relationship forged between Shy Boy and me as "catastrophic bonding." This is what often takes place when planes crash in mountainous terrain or hikers get lost in the backcountry. Instinctively, people come together in the face of grave danger. It seems, whether human or animal, we understand the value of the herd mentality when our life is perceived to be at risk. I fell in love with Shy Boy during those days of creating the documentary. I suppose I could say that catastrophic bonding affected me, too. I have felt an inordinate closeness to this horse every day since.

After the BBC left California, I took Shy Boy to one of my students, Ron Ralls, for training as a working cow horse while I traveled the world promoting *The Man Who Listens to Horses*. Shy Boy took his lessons well and became an even-tempered, cooperative equine student.

During my book tour, I was often asked about Shy Boy. People wanted to know where he was and how he was doing. Many asked what I thought he would do if I took him back out to the wilderness and released him with the same herd of horses. My answer was that I didn't know. I wasn't aware that anyone had ever tried such a thing before, so no one could really know the answer. But I was interested to find out. Eleven months after my first adventure with Shy Boy, we set out to film another documentary.

The plan was to return to the place where the first documentary had been done, release Shy Boy when we found his herd, and witness his response. I was convinced the other horses would kick him out immediately. He had been eating domestic feed and drinking water from a different area, and his body would give off a totally different scent from that of the family group he'd left behind.

I was wrong. They took him back as if he'd been away for just a day. Not one of them said a negative word to him. It was about three o'clock in the afternoon when we released him, and by dark he was miles from us with his herd. I told everyone in the film group that he would either come back in the night or first thing in the morning. I felt certain we would see him around our camp-site at dawn.

I was wrong again. At daylight he was nowhere to be seen. But at about nine o'clock the following morning he turned up on top of a hill about a quarter mile from our location. He stopped for a few seconds, looked back at the other horses, and then cantered down the hill directly to me. It was one of the most moving expe-riences of my career.

Shy Boy was home to stay and has never been away from us since that moment. He lives with us on Flag Is Up Farms, and I feel certain he believes he owns the place. He has his own box stall for sleeping and a field for daily turnout. He is visited by literally hundreds of people every week.

The wonderful little American mustang's regular job is to escort young horses to and from the riding arenas and training track on our farm. He shows young thoroughbreds how to go through the starting gate and is quite capable of assisting young cutting horses and reined cow horses in controlling the cattle they are working.

In 2003 Shy Boy led five newly trained wild mustangs in the Rose Parade. All six horses completed the chaotic five-mile route amid bands playing, people cheering, fireworks exploding, and low-flying aircraft passing overhead without a single negative step. Shy Boy seemed to know he had done a good job when we arrived at the schoolyard at the end of Colorado Boulevard, the designated finishing point for the equestrian participants. Even though it was a long night before and a grueling day, he seemed to have more spring in his step than any of the other horses. He seemed to want to be ridden in and around the others just to let them know that he was a proud teacher. I was proud of them all, but particularly Shy Boy.

Shy Boy has a home here for the rest of his life, and my relationship with him is as close as I've had with any horse. He is one of the gentlest horses on the face of this earth and a great tribute to those survivors of the early Spanish settlers in the western part of the United States.

READER/CUSTOMER CARE SURVEY

UHFG

We care about your opinions! Please take a moment to fill out our online Reader Survey at **http://survey.hcibooks.com.**
As a **"THANK YOU"** you will receive a **VALUABLE INSTANT COUPON** towards future book purchases
as well as a **SPECIAL GIFT** available only online! Or, you may mail this card back to us.

(PLEASE PRINT IN ALL CAPS)

First Name _____ MI. _____ Last Name _____

Address _____ City _____

State _____ Zip _____ Email _____

1. Gender
❏ Female   ❏ Male

2. Age
❏ 8 or younger
❏ 9-12   ❏ 13-16
❏ 17-20   ❏ 21-30
❏ 31+

3. Did you receive this book as a gift?
❏ Yes   ❏ No

4. Annual Household Income
❏ under $25,000
❏ $25,000 - $34,999
❏ $35,000 - $49,999
❏ $50,000 - $74,999
❏ over $75,000

5. What are the ages of the children living in your house?
❏ 0 - 14   ❏ 15+

6. Marital Status
❏ Single
❏ Married
❏ Divorced
❏ Widowed

7. How did you find out about the book?
(please choose one)
❏ Recommendation
❏ Store Display
❏ Online
❏ Catalog/Mailing
❏ Interview/Review

8. Where do you usually buy reading about books?
(please choose one)
❏ Bookstore
❏ Online
❏ Book Club/Mail Order
❏ Price Club (Sam's Club, Costco's, etc.)
❏ Retail Store (Target, Wal-Mart, etc.)

9. What attracts you most to a book?
(please choose one)
❏ Title
❏ Cover Design
❏ Author
❏ Content

10. What subject do you enjoy reading about the most?
(please choose one)
❏ Parenting/Family
❏ Relationships
❏ Recovery/Addictions
❏ Health/Nutrition
❏ Christianity
❏ Spirituality/Inspiration
❏ Business Self-help
❏ Women's Issues
❏ Sports
❏ Pets

TAPE IN MIDDLE; DO NOT STAPLE

FOLD HERE

The ULTIMATE Series

Comments

The paint horse was introduced to North America by the Spanish conquistadors.

Ah, the good life. A good friend, green grass. Doesn't get better than this.

Ah, life on the ranch.

Even horses that appear white are usually classified as gray.

This colt is displaying the flehman response, trying to discern a funny smell.

English riders use two-handed reigns and often side in a gentle snaffle bit.

Lip service. When grazing, horses use their lips to sort through the grass.

Can you keep a secret?

A Belgian Draft Horse Named Clyde

By Rolland Love

I tossed and turned in a sweat-soaked bed. It seemed I'd slept only a couple hours when dad opened the bedroom door.

Dad clapped his hands. "Up an' at 'em, Tommy. We've got a day's work to do."

I picked up a corner of the bedsheet and wiped sweat from my eyes. It had been a hot, sticky night, and I woke each time the grandfather clock in the living room chimed every hour on the hour. If my mom's dad hadn't given her the clock, I would have gotten out of bed and destroyed the chimer.

I looked out the window at the blazing orange fireball rising over the top of the hay barn. I could tell it was going to be another day when the temperature hovered at about 100 degrees.

"Breakfast is ready," Mom yelled from the kitchen. "Get your teenage tail in here. Your dad wants that hay hauled in today. It's supposed to rain."

I hopped to the floor, grabbed a pair of bib overalls from a chair, and pulled them on. I slipped into a long-sleeved blue denim work shirt and wiggled my feet into my high-top work shoes. Long sleeves were the order of the day when putting up hay to keep itchy alfalfa seeds off sweat-soaked skin.

I smiled to myself as I headed down the stairs, only one more workday in the hay field and then it would be the Fourth of July. I had saved my money and bought five dollar's worth of fireworks—mostly M-80s, which were powerful enough to blow a can into the air the height of a sycamore.

"You be careful with those firecrackers," Mom said as I walked into the kitchen, where she had a plate of biscuits and gravy and a glass of milk waiting.

"You know I will." I sat and forked a gravy-covered biscuit into my mouth.

"Your dad's finished breakfast. He's outside hitching Clyde to the wagon. You should finish hayin' today. Then you can start choppin' down those sprouts."

I so hated the thought of digging out sprouts that I pretended I hadn't heard what she said. Clyde was our big chestnut Belgian draft horse who did many different jobs around the farm. Sometimes I rode him along the river. He was a good swimmer and loved the water. I felt bad that he had to work so hard and figured he hated the heat as much as I did.

We were into our fifth day of work to put up twenty-five acres of alfalfa. During the last four days, Clyde had pulled the sickle mower to cut the hay. While it lay in the field, drying in the sun, Dad worked Clyde in the woods, hauling out logs he had cut from a dozen oak trees to sell to the sawmill.

When the hay was dry, Clyde pulled a ten-foot-wide dump rake. Its long, curved steel tongs, mounted on a frame set between two wheels, swept the hay into rows. Today, Clyde would pull the wagon while we used a pitchfork to toss the hay onto a flatbed to haul it to the barn. There, we'd use a hayfork that looked like a giant set of metal ice tongs to lift it inside.

After I gobbled down breakfast and gave Mom a peck on the cheek, I met Dad at the wagon. We headed for the hayfield down in the river bottom.

As the sun blazed, Dad got on one side of the wagon and I got on the other. Clyde started down the first hay row with only a "Giddy up!" from Dad. The old horse slowly walked across the field, and when Dad said, "Whoa!" Clyde stopped.

At first, people didn't believe Clyde would do such a thing as pull the wagon without a driver. But after folks like Preacher Roberts and Mr. Simpson, the banker, saw it firsthand, nobody doubted Clyde anymore.

After we'd lifted the second load of hay off the wagon and into the barn we stopped for lunch. I led Clyde to a water trough in the shade of a big oak tree, scooped up a bucketful of water, splashed some on the horse's neck, and rubbed the white froth off his skin.

I glanced over my shoulder to make sure nobody was looking and got close to Clyde's big, old ears. "I love you, Clyde. I wish you didn't have to work in the hot sun."

He turned his head and gave me a nudge, and I looked into his big, brown eyes. I know it was all in my mind, but I had no doubt that he understood what I said.

Grandpa Tom and Grandma Mary joined us for lunch, and I was glad because Grandma baked the best apple pies. A brown-crusted one oozing gooey cinnamon sauce from the top was on the table. There was also a heap of fried chicken on a big white platter, a bowl of potato salad, and a pitcher of lemonade. Grandpa blessed it all. After lunch it was off to one of the shade trees in the yard for a thirty-minute snooze. We headed back to the field knowing the workday was half done.

At the end of the day, the hay was out of the field and in the barn. It was enough to feed twenty head of Hereford cattle, a milk cow, and a couple of goats for the winter. I led Clyde out into the pond and splashed cool water on his back. He turned his head toward me and rubbed his soft, pink nose on my neck.

With our work behind us, my mind filled with thoughts of the Fourth of July and blowin' things up, right and left, with my powerful M-80s. After the holiday, the next hot job would be chopping sprouts with a broad-head ax. It was amazing how many tree saplings grew back from year to year. If we didn't keep the crop chopped, eventually it would take over and cover much-needed grazing land. What kept me going while chopping the sprouts—a job I hated—was the fact that Clyde got a little time off. There was no man or beast who deserved it more.

A Winning End

By Kathleen Livingston

After fifteen years as a winning show horse, reiner, working cow horse, halter horse, English pleasure horse, and trail horse, it was time to pass the torch. In that time, our best friend, MHR Star Spangled, had also served as a working ranch horse, breeding stallion, and our kids' taxi. It was time to allow him to retire.

The gate of the indoor arena at Denver's National Western Complex opened and our horse entered. His relaxed presence assured all onlookers that he knew what he was doing. The gate closed behind him. My husband, Cody, merely directed our trusted mount toward the far end of the arena, where a cow would enter. Our horse stood quiet, ears forward, eyes steady, relaxed, and ready. Cody nodded. Both horse and rider waited only moments for the cow to be released into the arena.

The clang of the shoot gate was immediately followed by the bold entrance of an Angus cow. The shoot gate closed, and the work began. Our horse's ears went back, almost becoming one with his neck. He parried and ducked, first right then left, then right and left again, thwarting the cow's attempt to get by him.

His longtime rider sat astride doing nothing more than maintaining his position in the saddle. Our well-trained and savvy horse was doing all the work.

Star Spangled, our gray stallion, held the cow at the end of the arena, showing the judge and onlookers that he can control a cow. Cody lightly pulled on the reins, checking the horse. Star Spangled hesitated in response to his rider's cue. The hesitation, although momentary, was enough to give the cow breathing room and an avenue of escape—an escape route planned and orchestrated by my husband, but an escape route nevertheless. The cow ran along the wall, down the length of the arena. Cody dropped his left hand less than an inch, and Star Spangled began to run. Gaining speed with ease and passing the cow, the horse instinctively turned into the fence, forcing the cow to turn and head back down the rail in the opposite direction. Our horse gained speed. Passing the cow, he got to its shoulder, leaned into it, took one more stride, and while going full tilt, without being told, turned left into the rail, causing the cow to come to a full stop. Spangled had gotten inside the cow's bubble. The cow turned around and attempted to get away from her imposing opponent again.

Cody softly shortened the length of his reins by less than an inch, cuing our horse to slow up and allow the cow to come off the rail. The duo brought the cow out into the center of the arena. Our gray stallion ran to the cow's shoulder, causing it to circle left. My husband did not discourage our horse's increased speed as he kept pace with the cow. Cody sat astride our surefooted mount at a dead run. A short, light pull on the reins slowed the horse only enough to let the cow get ahead of them. Then they switched to the cow's left side. Within two strides Star Spangled was able to run up to the cow's left shoulder and they circled her to the left.

Satisfied that the required elements of the class had been completed within the two and a half minutes allowed, Cody lightly and steadily pulled on the reins, telling our horse to stop. The constant light pressure on the reins and a gentle clicking noise signaled Spangled to back three steps. Then the reins lay loose on the stallion's neck. Spangled had finished his work. Whistling, clapping, and whoops—in addition to those I was sending up from my place at the rail—were a clear indication that the crowd liked our working cow horse and his performance.

Cody lifted his right hand to the brim of his silver Stetson and tipped it to the crowd as he allowed the gray stallion to walk out of the arena on a loose rein like an old broke ranch horse. I watched Spangled exit with his neck slightly arched, his head set steady in the bridle, tail up, loose reins swaying back and forth in cadence with his comfortable gait.

"That was a good work, old man!" Cody said, patting our horse on the right hip as they passed through the open gate.

"Did you hear the score?" he asked me once they were out of the arena.

"No," I said as I reached up and stroked the old gray on the neck. "But it is a work to be proud of." The smile that covered my face included a sparkle of sadness in my eyes.

We waited with the other competitors until all of the horses had worked. The animals stood relaxed. We all waited and listened for the announcer.

"We'd like to call all of the bitted working cow horses back into the arena," a voice boomed over the public-address system. The competitors assembled side by side in the arena. "We would like to present your 1998 Region Eight purebred Arabian bitted working cow horse champion, with a score of 71.5 points . . . number 511, MHR Star Spangled by Bay El Bey and out of Star of Bask, owned and ridden by Cody Walton of Florence, Colorado!"

Cody's face glowed with pride. He picked up his split reins with his left hand, patted Star Spangled on the right hip with his right, and said, "Not a bad way to end your career, son," a touch of regret tingeing his words.

Star Spangled walked forward until a young girl presenting the ribbons came toward him. Without a cue from his rider, Star Spangled stopped and dropped his head as the little blond draped the blue, red, and yellow championship ribbon around his neck. Then she handed Cody a wooden plaque and trophy adorned with a brass image of an Arabian horse's head and neck. She also secured a maroon and pink Region Eight champion ribbon to the buckle of the horse's breast collar at his left shoulder. The rosette-topped ribbon covered the point of his shoulder with wide streamers that hung three-fourths of the way down his forearm.

Ears forward, adorned in ribbons, Star Spangled could not have looked more majestic.

"Congratulations," Bill, a fellow competitor from Utah, said to me.

"Thanks. Not bad for nineteen years old, huh?" I said, not taking my eyes off our gray.

Cody headed Star Spangled around the arena at a gentle canter for the customary winner's lap as the announcer repeated his name and his accomplishment. Cody cued the horse for a sliding stop before they exited the arena at a walk.

As we headed back to the stall, we heard the announcer add, "You are all invited to Star Spangled's retirement ceremony and party. It begins at 1 PM in the warm-up arena."

We let Star Spangled rest before I bathed him and readied him for the ceremony.

The arena wall was lined with spectators. Some had seen Spangled perform many times and in many places over the last fifteen years, others were just lucky enough to watch a good horse today. Star Spangled sauntered into the warm-up arena with his long-time owner, trainer, and rider up. Cody began to put the horse through his paces. Cueing Spangled into a canter, they traveled in a figure eight, flawlessly exhibiting flying lead changes, spins, and a couple deep and straight sliding stops. The choreographed moves we had planned were performed to the carefully picked theme song of the *Highlander* TV series. I watched as they stopped in the middle of the arena as the music changed to a slow instrumental piece also by Queen.

Cody dismounted, letting both split reins drop to the ground. Our seven-year-old son walked to his father and handed him a set of long-handled nippers. Then he stood, shoulders back, head held high, with the leather reins draped in his hands.

"Give us," Cody said as he reached down for the horse's right front hoof. Star Spangled responded by lifting it and balancing his weight on his other three legs. Holding the hoof between his knees, Cody pulled the iron shoe. Setting the hoof down, he moved to the left side. Before touching the leg he said, "Give us," again. The second shoe was pulled, but not before Cody paused to whip a tear and collect himself.

"Cody pulls the shoes of this horse in the old-time ranch tradition of pulling the shoes of one's good retiring horses," the announcer read the explanation I had written as spectators watched in awed silence.

Cody handed the nippers and shoes to our son, then stepped up and unsaddled his friend as our five-year-old daughter entered the arena with a garland of silk roses in her hands. Now the horse's cinch and latigo were hanging loose, and Cody fastened the gift around our gray's neck.

"Kathleen is entering the arena with WA Walking Tall, a son of Star Spangled. Tonight, Star Spangled will be handing over his legacy to his son who, with the grace of Allah, will be able to carry on in the same fashion of his sire," the announcer read from the script. I stopped our younger, steel-gray stallion in front of his sire. I allowed the two to stand face-to-face. Gazing at them, I was confident their conformation would leave no question that they were father and son even to strangers leaning on the rail.

We saddled Walking Tall as our assistant brought our two-year-old daughter to us. I put a lead loosely around Star Spangled's neck so I could unbridle him. I slid the crownpiece over his ears, and he allowed the spade bit to drop out of his mouth. Casually, I brought the black patent-leather halter up over his muzzle and up over his velvety ears, allowing the lead to fall to the ground. I placed the bridle and reins over my shoulder.

While Cody was tightening the girth on Tall, I lifted the children up onto Star Spangled's bare back. First Ethan up front, then Elantra, and lastly I put Kayla up in the back.

The powerful beats of the *Highlander* theme song began again, and our family walked out of the arena, wiping tears from our eyes as the soundtrack said, "I am immortal, I have inside me the blood of kings."

Surrogacy Ain't Fer Sissies

By Kathe Campbell

As we awaited a blessed event, Mother Nature sent us clouds and lower temperatures, a nice relief from the Montana summer heat. My husband, Ken, and I had raised some world-class donkey stock, but as yet, no spotted babies. Duns and blacks graced our acres, but spots so far had eluded our dreams.

It had crossed my mind to confine Blossom, our black brood jennet, to the corral Saturday night because her udder had been tight that afternoon. There were no signs of waxing, so I changed my mind, knowing full well she would do the sensible thing and return to her stall to foal. We were eagerly awaiting this baby because the sire was a mammoth spotted jack.

Daybreak on Sunday found Ken searching the closet for his heavy flannel shirt, wool socks, and snow boots. I pulled the quilt over my head to shut out his grumbling as he headed out the door to feed. Eight inches of August snow covered the pastures, and the whiteout conditions made it seem like February. It was nearly thirty-five degrees at this hour, but the windchill lowered the temperature considerably. Fir boughs bent over double strained fences and power lines. Even more worrisome, Blossom was nowhere to

be found. Ken called and called, but her off-key excuse for a bray
was not forthcoming, so he hotfooted it into the woods.

After searching wildly, Ken heard a piercing chorus of hee-
haws and whistles down in the gully and he broke into a run.
Nearly invisible through the giant white flakes stood the ladies-
in-waiting, lending support to Blossom and her newly arrived
foal. Newborns can handle low temperatures, but they are ill
equipped to deal with wet and cold. Hypothermia is a wicked
killer. Blossom's warm massages must have been the only thing
keeping the baby on his feet. It was snowing harder than she
could lick away the flakes.

At first Ken was furious with the jennet for pulling such a
stunt, but the sight of the wet foal peaked his adrenaline and
melted his heart. On the spot he named the youngster August
Storm to reflect the wrath of the day. Then he swept the foal into
his arms and, with Blossom dogging his every step, headed for our
warm basement. The months of waiting were nothing compared
to the trial of clambering back up the slick hill and getting the
soaking wet newborn to a warm, dry place.

"He's spotted, Kathe, a spotted jack!"

Ken excitedly whipped open the linen-closet doors and
grabbed every towel in sight. While I hurriedly pulled on my
boots, I agreed that even the towels with the hand-embroidered
ducks weren't good enough for this wish-come-true. Sure enough,
as I quietly peeked into the makeshift nursery, there stood one
beautiful jack, our biggest foal yet. He sported soft, muted tricolored spots, a beautiful head, and perfect legs. While loading in
bales of straw, I briefly reflected on Blossom's twelve months of

gestation—one month longer than horses are pregnant. The extra time is needed, of course, to produce those magnificent long ears.

Blossom's huge brown eyes grew wild with fury at the sight of towels swishing back and forth over Storm's shivering frame. The baby began to sneeze and cough, sending us into a tailspin. I briefly thought of the hair dryer, but temporarily abandoned the idea. If we could only get the little guy to suck, it would do wonders. Mother and child had probably braved the elements most of the night. They both were shaking as Storm collapsed onto the bed of straw. Blossom made it clear she wanted privacy with her baby.

Around 10 AM, we again opened the doors and felt Storm's new little muscles beginning to relax. Oh dear Lord, I silently prayed, give us all strength to bring this beautiful tyke through. Over and over again Blossom nudged her foal, urging him to stand. Finally, she hovered directly over him, encouraging him to suck. But her determination was fading as her frustration grew.

By noon Blossom's milk was streaming with her every move. The phone was ringing with neighbors lamenting the power outage and the local horsey set was peering in from the doorway, lending words of encouragement and occasionally some bad advice. Questions arose about the dark, crosslike stripe that ran down the foal's back and across his withers. In response, I issued my usual words of wisdom, "What did Mary ride to Bethlehem?"

Ken felt that Storm was on the verge of serious trouble and I was scolding myself for not locking his mother in. At the risk of offending our well-meaning neighbors, he invited them to close the door as they left because it was now time for us to swing into action.

Over Blossom's verbal protests, I secured her to some support posts just as she managed a well-placed kick. None of our donkey family had ever taken aim at us, but this episode scarcely counted. Once again, Ken swept Storm into his arms and sat down directly under Blossom's flanks. He held up the foal's tiny chin, hoping the youngster would realize that the best part of being a baby was right there in front of him. Realize it he did and within minutes he was guzzling his first breakfast with gusto. Blossom was released and her entire body relaxed. Although I'm sure she would never admit it, she was grateful. Ken heaved a huge sigh, and as usual at critter crisis time, I streamed happy tears.

In those critical hours, Storm's tail had not emerged once from between his precious hind legs, but now here it was, flicking in obvious joy while he filled his gullet to overflowing. No thanks to Montana's unpredictability, August Storm was off to a splendid start.

Take a Chance

By Chera Cluck as told to Carrie Pepper

I t was one of those days when it took everything I had to get out of bed. My schedule as a horse trainer kept me at the track seven days a week, and I was exhausted. But I was also too stubborn and in love with my horses to take time off, and I soon discovered the real reason I was at Santa Anita that morning.

On May 12, 2007, I was busy with my chores: taking temperatures, checking legs, picking the stalls, making sure all my horses were getting the best care. I had just gone out to dump my muck cart when something extraordinary happened.

I had no idea that one of the horses at the track, a five-year-old named Take a Chance, had gone down during his morning workout. The ambulance passed by slowly, and I could see a horse in the back. He was a beautiful bay with pricked-up ears, and he looked too happy and alive to die. I soon learned he had suffered a multiple fracture in his right front leg. It was a very bad break.

A brigade filed past. First, the ambulance followed by the vet, and then security personnel. I knew what was about to happen and I felt compelled to do something right away. I had to find out if the horse's life could be saved.

By the time I arrived at the blue room, where horses are euthanized, everyone was there. When I asked, "Can he be saved?" the security guard's face went blank.

Was it too late? I thought.

The vet appeared from the back stall where he was treating Chance and answered, "Yes, he can be saved." But he had already given Chance the first shot to relax him; the next one would put him down. He was a dead horse on paper, and the green wagon was on the way.

My heart pounded as the vet went on to explain that the surgeon's fee would be $1,500 and more expenses would follow. Horses give us their absolute all, and I would have sold everything I had to save Take a Chance. I knew I couldn't let him die. I had seen him around the backstretch. He had a zest for life that was still obvious when I glimpsed him through the ambulance window.

I begged the vet to work with me. I assured him I'd find the money. He waited as I called a good friend. The vet spoke with her, and she agreed to guarantee the money needed for Chance's surgery. My next call was to the stable superintendent who, among other things, is responsible for documenting incidents on track property. Chance's owner had signed the paperwork for euthanasia, giving the track responsibility for the horse's disposition. I explained what was happening, and the superintendent agreed to our plan to keep Chance alive.

Over the next few days, donations poured in for food and bedding, and several nonprofit organizations came forward with offers to sponsor Chance. He was a stakes winner with winnings in excess of $100,000. This champion horse was popular.

One group, the Exceller Fund, offered to donate the money for Chance's surgery. The reason was not because he had competed in racing's higher ranks; it was because it was simply the right thing to do. Established in 1997 by a group of horse lovers, the fund is dedicated to providing thoroughbred racehorses with a future beyond the finish line. In particular, it strives to save them from the sort of terrible fate that Exceller faced. A successful racehorse and sire in the late-1970s and mid-1980s, he was sent to slaughter in Europe in 1997 when his bankrupt owner decided the horse was no longer of value. At age twenty-three, Exceller was not ill or injured; as a stallion, he was still able to get mares in foal. But none of that mattered. At the time of his death, his name was on the ballot for the National Thoroughbred Racing Hall of Fame. He earned a spot there in 1999.

I was especially grateful for the Exceller Fund's offer.

Five days later, Chance was in a padded room, where he was sedated and gently placed on an operating table. My sister, Susanne, joined me for moral support. We were pony buddies as kids and Susanne still shared my love for horses. While Chance was prepped for surgery, his sweet eyes were free of fear, as if he knew we were all his trusted friends.

The condition of the leg was worse than we expected, with bone fragments everywhere. But the procedure went smoothly, and I think the surgeon was guided from above. I don't think it was a coincidence that the day Chance was injured, May 12, also was Exceller's birthday.

Bonnie Mizrahi, president of the Exceller Fund, explained that a group known as the Fans of Barbaro—the horse who suffered a catastrophic injury in the 2006 Kentucky Derby—thought of Chance as a Barbaro Junior, but with a happier ending. Their generosity at the time of his surgery saved Chance, and now their monthly donations help provide for his care. The Southern California Equine Foundation through a sister organization, the Dolly Green Research Foundation, covered facility costs and supplies. The surgeon, Joe Morgan, D.V.M., and anesthesiologist, Dr. Cathy Canfield, donated their services.

One of the conditions for support from the Southern California Equine Foundation required that Chance's papers be turned in to the Jockey Club marked "sold without pedigree." This ensures that when Chance is adopted, his new owners will not be able to race him.

With the approval of the stable superintendent, Chance recovered from surgery in my barn at the track. After six weeks of TLC there, he was transported to Tranquility Farm, an equestrian rehabilitation facility in Tehachapi, California. The owner, Pricilla Clark, says he's a friendly, happy horse who is up all the time. He loves to play and is always willing to interact with people. He's going to make a great horse for the right adopter.

Chance is alive today because of the compassion of the stable superintendent, the skill and care of many veterinarians and their staff, and the generosity of horse lovers who became aware of his struggle. He is living proof that there are other options besides euthanasia for some injured horses.

I close my eyes and I'm standing alongside the rail at Santa Anita. The buzzer rings *and they're off!* I hear their thunder as they round the track, giving their riders the best they have, running flat out. They run for us.

Chance grazes in a green field at Tranquility Farm as he waits for his new owners. In his heart, he imagines his wild ancestors on the plains, running free without restraint, unbridled through juniper and sagebrush in wild open spaces. He remembers the joy of racing. He remembers going down. I pray he'll always remember someone who loved him enough to take a chance on him.

A Lifetime of Love

By Sarah K. Andrew

Alibar is twenty-nine and I am thirty. We have been together most of our lives, and although my life has changed much since we met, he has always been Alibar, my sidekick and friend.

He has led me on my life's trail. My passion for equine photography started with him as my first subject. My work is all about admiring and celebrating horses, but it also forces me to understand their fragility and how few lead a life like Alibar's. I know how special it is that I have had him for so long, and I sense that he, too, understands this in his own way.

I met Alibar when he was ten years old and I was eleven.

I was a typical horseless, horse-crazy little girl, raised on a steady diet of riding lessons, Sam Savitt drawings, and Breyer model horses. My mother and grandmother encouraged me with stories of moonlight trail rides and chapters of *National Velvet*. I named my mom's canaries after the lesson ponies I had ridden. When I was not riding, I was setting up elaborate jumper courses for the neighborhood dogs. My bicycle was a chestnut thoroughbred mare named Foxy. My teachers begged me to stop writing book reports about the Black Stallion series.

The night before I met Alibar, I slept with my bridle in my bed, dreaming of a horse who was as fast as the wind and could jump the moon. My mother's friend, Diane, had invited us to come see her horse. Alibhai's Alibar was a registered appaloosa with no spots, sickle hocks, a bull neck, and a frizzy tuft of hair where a forelock should be. Diane bought Alibar when he was a weanling, and she nicknamed him Baby Brat for his headstrong nature and tendency to run off with his riders.

My grandmother was in the market for a dressage horse, but Alibar wasn't right. No one was looking to buy him, so I rode him for the rest of the summer. When I returned to school, my projects and papers were all about Alibar. I wrote about him in Latin class, photographed his nose for a school publication, drew pictures of him in art class, and even based my science project on the equine center of gravity.

In the end, it became clear that we belonged together, and so it was.

Alibar is the fastest horse I've ever ridden. When we gallop, tears stream from my eyes and the wind screams in my ears. We raced many horses over the years and never were beaten. His speed, combined with his catty agility, gave him fantastic jumping ability. His natural impulsion made jumping a thrill. We started by trotting over homemade jump poles and then graduated to cross-rails with truck tires, traffic cones, and cinder blocks as standards. Then I fashioned verticals and oxers out of the same materials. We rode on hunter paces and successfully competed in local horse shows.

Alibar was fifteen and I was sixteen when I broke my collarbone.

One February afternoon, we were taking a spin around the soccer field when he slid on the grass. Beneath a deep layer of grass and mud, the ground was frozen, and his feet simply lost their grip. He scrambled to stay upright, but landed on his left side, with me still in the saddle. We slid about fifteen feet. Alibar quickly rolled upright off my leg and was already standing as I got to my feet. I carefully checked his legs and felt his sides for injuries. He was shaken but fine. My own arm was dangling, the collarbone broken. I hooked my arm into my jacket sleeve and held it with my other arm, leaving Alibar's reins free. Over the soccer field, down the sand pits, and through the neighborhood, he dutifully walked by my side all the way back to the barn.

Alibar was twenty-two and I was twenty-three when he started having problems with his feet.

I was afraid I'd lose my riding partner, so I decided to take the opportunity to reschool him and retrain myself as a rider. I pulled out my dressage books, and we started anew. I reevaluated my riding and spent a lot of time refining my legs, seat, and hands. As I improved my skills, Alibar no longer pulled on my hands or needed a severe bit. His canter became light and springy.

Alibar was twenty-seven and I was twenty-eight when we competed in our first horse show after a nine-year hiatus. He performed gamely, and I was proud to show off his blue ribbons back at the barn.

And now we are here, the current juncture of our lives.

He is still teaching, and I am still learning. He is toothless, sometimes silly. He will mug for doughnuts and still kicks up his heels on a breezy spring day. He loves to learn tricks and picks them up quickly.

He is the only horse I have ever owned, and although I now photograph horses far more famous—Kentucky Derby winners and top eventing horses, world-class dressage stallions, and horses worth millions—he is still my favorite subject when I look through my lens.

Alibar is twenty-nine and I am thirty. I know there won't be many more years for him and I try not to think about it much. He is my horse, my one horse, and I've never outgrown him. His life is nearly over, and mine is just entering its prime.

But he has carried me this far and I know he will carry me forever.

Alibar lived a happy life
with photographer Sarah Andrew
until the age of twenty-nine.

Horses have numerous muscles in the ears, allowing them to swivel them to sounds of interest.

A dapple gray,
striking a pose.

I like to dress for
the occasion.

Are you in charge of mice
control around here?

A newborn getting
used to his legs.

The appaloosa is a breed developed in North America by the Nez Perce tribe.

A gorgeous chestnut.

Red-Carpet Treatment

By Cary Davis

Rolling out the red carpet is usually reserved for welcoming celebrities and dignitaries. When movie stars set foot on the red runway it's all about watching the best, brightest, and most beautiful. When horses crave the spotlight, it can be a different story.

Like people, some horses have mischievous personalities. Scooter, a five-year-old chestnut quarter horse gelding, was that way. His owner boarded him at my place and had warned me about his need for fun and games. Like a happy security guard with a sense of humor, Scooter patrolled the paddock daily looking for entertaining ways to pass the time. Rattling grain buckets that were hanging on the fence, playing tug-of-war with a turnout buddy, or carrying a stick in his mouth were some of his favorites.

One day, in a hurry before leaving for a business meeting, I quickly glanced at the horses to check on them and saw they were snoozing peacefully in the noonday sun. As I turned to pick up my briefcase and head for the door, something red caught my eye at the far end of the paddock. I stopped and stared in the direction of the bright color. What could it be? What was hanging over the fence? Then it occurred to me. My nonhorsey neighbors recently had returned from a long summer vacation and must have been cleaning house. They had hung two rugs over the top rail, probably to knock off the dust.

So now I had a dilemma. I weighed my options and decided to leave the rugs where they were so I wouldn't risk getting my clothes dirty or being late for my meeting. I rationalized that I wouldn't be gone for very long and the horses were napping. What could possibly happen?

When I returned a few hours later and looked out toward the turnout area, there was Scooter standing center stage with all eyes on him. He had literally rolled out the red carpet. He was standing on one of the rugs, which he had dragged to his favorite rolling spot. The other dangled from his mouth. It was large, approximately three feet by five feet, and he held it by one end and tossed his head up and down, causing the rug to flip up and hit him. Then he'd shake and twirl it before tossing it over his back. The carpet was big enough that it completely covered his head a few times. When that happened, he stopped moving for a moment and his audience of two geldings, mesmerized by his act, moved in closer, encouraging him to start the show again.,

I watched all of this play out and I couldn't help but laugh. At the same time, I was concerned about him harming my neighbor's floor coverings. I headed out to the paddock, hollering, "Scooter, drop it!" He immediately turned to look at me, his eyes dancing with delight. I repeated my instructions and he spit out his toy. As it fell, it produced a large puff of dust, creating a smoke-and-mirrors effect for his stage show.

As I tried to muffle my laughter I said, "Very bad Scooter. Step away from the rug." He just stood there watching me approach, still standing on the Southwestern-style carpet. The other two horses slowly started backing away from the scene of the crime. It was as if they wanted to put some distance between themselves and Scooter to make it known that they were simply innocent bystanders. They were clearly pointing the hoof at the bad guy and their behavior was almost as funny as his.

Scooter was happy to see me but confused as to why I had closed his one-man show on opening night. I patted the little clown as I picked up the goods to assess the damage. The fringe on one end of the rug he was standing on had been torn off completely. There was a large rip and a hole near the center where he had unraveled the wool fabric. The rug he had been tossing had fared better. However, both pieces were covered with slobber and dust.

As I searched the area for rug residue, Scooter followed me, curious to see if playtime would resume. His comedy show had now become the mysterious red carpet caper. I combed the corral but could not find the missing pieces of fringe or material. I was baffled. The rugs definitely showed signs of foul play. So where were the remnants? Then I began to worry. What if clown boy had swallowed the evidence? I put my fears of colic aside and realized the puzzle was not going to be solved that evening.

I struggled as I thought about what I should do. My neighbors were not home when the incident occurred, and I had to leave again to give a riding lesson. I decided I would knock off as much dirt as possible, put the rugs back on the fence, and then give them a little shove as if the wind had blown them down or the horses had gently nudged them while investigating. I felt guilty but at the time didn't know how else to handle the situation. It didn't help that the audience members were still standing several paces back, watching with judgmental looks on their faces.

For the next few days I was a nervous Nellie, expecting my neighbors to knock on the door and demand reparation for the destruction of their prized family heirlooms. They did appear, but not to register dismay. Instead they invited me to their home for dinner. My guilt over Scooter's escapade was still eating at me. *Oh sure*, I thought. *They'll pour me a glass of wine and then present me with an itemized invoice.*

Several days later, I arrived at their home for what was my first visit. As I approached the porch, I realized the steps were covered by the rug Scooter had stood on. The missing fringe and other battle scars were still evident. Then I walked into the kitchen and saw the smaller rug in front of the sink.

I took a deep breath. This was going to be a long evening. As I was led into the dining area and living room, my neighbors began pointing out all the furnishings they had picked up at local yard sales, explaining how some things came with blemishes, showing signs of previous wear, but they didn't mind. To them, it was an affordable, fun way to furnish their home.

In the end, I realized Scooter had not caused as much damage as I had originally thought. In fact, the neighbors were completely unaware that their rugs had been rolled out for a brief, VIP—very important pony—red carpet treatment.

Our Playful Paint

By Jennifer DiCamillo

D ay One: The weather in southern Missouri had been beautiful, nothing but pleasing breezes and sunny skies. My greatest joy was looking out my kitchen window to the pasture to see my two horses munching long stalks of plentiful grass hay.

I opened the screen and inhaled. Fresh air washed over me, and I could hear the joyful sounds of my children—all teenagers—playing on the trampoline that was out in the field. Life in the country didn't get any better than Highlandville, Missouri. It was close enough to bigger towns for convenience and far enough out to feel separated from all the hustle and bustle of modern society.

Day Two: The kids were driving me crazy. They seemed to be underfoot all the time. When I no longer could take it, I yelled to them, "All of you, out the door, run around the property! If you come back, I'm gonna put you to work!"

The threat of chores had them moving in no time.

We have acres and acres so they can run. It keeps them fit and healthy, gives them time to commune a little with nature, and provides me with some peace and quiet—usually.

This day they weren't gone more than two minutes before the

sound of wailing drifted in through the kitchen window. I was afraid to go out to look.

"Oh God," I prayed, "please don't let one of my horses be down or dead. I just couldn't deal with that today."

I don't handle that sort of thing well on any day. But the crying and groaning didn't die down. So as a good mother and responsible pet owner, I headed outside to see what was wrong. Surely no one had had time to break an arm or leg on the trampoline. Up went another prayer as I went outside.

Nope. God had heard my pleas. All the animals were alive and kicking—fortunately, not at the kids, who were all fine, too.

The trampoline, however, looked like it had been hit by a tornado. No wonder the kids were wailing.

"The trampoline is ruined!" one cried the moment she saw me.

"Please don't make me clean the toilet," said another. "I hate to do the bathroom!"

I blinked between them, took a look for myself, and was flabbergasted at the trampoline's mangled appearance. There had been no storm in the night. We live in a hollow, and the wind rarely reaches us. What on earth could have happened to it?

By some miracle of manpower, my husband untangled the thing and got it operational before sundown. He was our hero, our champion, and the highest bouncer in the whole family. The world was good again.

Day Three: A repeat of the day before. I sent the kids out and, once again, the trampoline was ruined. This time, the horses were sniffing around it, and we had to move them to another field. We didn't want one of them tripping over a piece of it and cutting an artery or poking out an eye.

Wonderman fixed it again. But he complained. "This trampo-line thing couldn't happen on its own." He eyed the kids as if he suspected one of them of mangling it on purpose.

Nevertheless, he and the children jumped for exercise and joy. Later, when he'd fed the animals their grain, my husband let the horses back into the field where the trampoline was.

Day Four: You got it. The trampoline was mauled by daybreak. No tornado had come through. No children had been outside.

We were really wondering what was going on. It would take a pretty good force to knock a trampoline sideways and then get it so out of whack that it looked ruined.

This time when my husband managed to put it back together, we didn't cheer. The kids didn't jump. We set up lawn chairs and stared at the thing. Of course, it didn't do anything. The sun went down, and we went in. The mystery of the mangled tramp haunted my dreams that night. After all, there were rumors of our little hollow being haunted.

Day Five: Up early, I went out to check the horses' water. As I rounded the corner of the house, I saw what had been happening to the trampoline.

Our dorky colt, a paint horse we called W.C. (and sometimes Butthead), was putting his front leg into the space between the springs—very daintily, I might add. He'd reach a hoof just over the bar then pull it back out. He did this over and over again, each time going a little farther with his hoof until he finally stood on it, straddling the outer bar of the trampoline. He looked supremely satisfied with himself—so much so that he lifted his nose and showed his teeth to the sky.

I couldn't believe my eyes. Then, as I watched, he decided he was done standing there and he began trying to lift his hoof out. He was having a hard time and had made several attempts before I could even make it to the gate to try to help. With 1,200 pounds of strength, he yanked and bucked and dragged the whole frame with him for a few feet. He did it again and managed to get free. As he ran off, he plowed his way over the downed section of the trampoline then bucked with both back feet in a truly liberating crow hop.

Silly horse. He knew he was in trouble by the way I'd started yelling. Now I was hollering for the kids to come outside quick. In my mind, I was calling for help. But in reality and retrospect, I realize I probably used the same tone that W.C. had heard a thousand times before when he'd put his nose into something he shouldn't.

He ran behind a tree. Not a whole tree, mind you. Just enough to hide his eye. The rest of him remained in plain sight. But he peeked at me as the kids came around the corner of the house.

"What happened?" My oldest daughter exclaimed when she saw the trampoline.

I put my hands on my hips and stated, "The bad kid who tore up the trampoline is hiding behind a tree. Can you guess who it is?"

He ducked again, probably in response to my tone.

We moved the trampoline out of the field that evening. But every time anyone jumped on it, W.C. ran to the fence, stomped his foot, and tossed his mane as if to say, *I want to play on that thing too!*

Unconditional Love

Always in the Ribbons

By Roberta Thomas Mancuso

Sure Ain't Misbehavin is a horse. But not just any horse. He's an American-bred quarter horse who gave this family a day we will never forget when we needed it most.

When he came into our lives, I was not planning on becoming a horse owner. As a child I had had a dream that I would some-day own a horse, but when the realities of adulthood set in, that dream quickly faded. However, when my young daughter caught the horse bug and turned out to be a pretty good rider, I knew that I wanted to make that dream come true for her.

From the time she was twelve through her teens, owning a horse became her mission and obsession. I would find little notes scribbled in the strangest places: "Mom, I'll do anything for a horse!" "Pleeeeeeeeese buy me a horse or I will die," and count-less other renditions of the same theme.

Finally, not wanting her to die of horselessness, her stepdad and I felt we were in the position financially to make owning a horse a reality for her. We bought some land where we could build a house and a barn with a pasture and a riding ring. A bonus was that our land was near miles of trails and other horse farms.

We set out to find the perfect horse, which was no easy task. There just weren't many stunners in our price range until we stumbled across an ad on the Internet. It read something like this: "Sure Ain't Misbehavin, beautiful 16.1-hand, registered chestnut quarter horse gelding, twelve years old. This horse goes both Western and English and is always in the ribbons. You can ride him every day or every six months and he is always the same great ride. You can put a two-year-old on him or an eighty-year-old and he is the perfect babysitter. Not spooky and great stable manners."

I wondered if he would cook our dinner and do the grocery shopping as well. The ad was clearly exaggerated in my mind, but we were getting low on options as Jessica was starting her sophomore year of high school and winter would soon be closing in. Every horse we had looked at so far had some kind of a problem. If she wanted to become acclimated to her new horse and get some riding time in, we needed to find something soon.

On the day we met Sure Ain't Misbehavin, or Howdy as he was nicknamed, we walked into the owner's barn and there, standing perfectly still on cross ties, was this stunning chestnut horse with a large star and a pink snip on his nose. I exchanged a quick look with Jess. Wow, this was some handsome horse. At least the first line of the ad was true.

Howdy was certainly a looker, but what kind of mount would he be? Our tryouts with him ended up going well. He vetted out, and we took him home within a month.

The first thing we did was change his name. For years Jessica had been collecting possible horse names in a file. There was even a website dedicated to horse names. In the end his new name was right in front of our noses. We took Sure Ain't Misbehavin and shortened it to Sam. It suited him well and he quickly learned to respond to it.

It's one thing to take lessons, ride your friend's horse, or take care of someone else's horses on their farm. It's an entirely different level of responsibility to have your own horse—a 1,200-pound creature—housed in your barn and relying on you for his existence. Luckily for us, we had several horse owners nearby who offered both help and advice, and it was all appreciated and needed.

Soon fall progressed to winter and Jessica was at school, rarely having time to ride. So I began the daily riding regimen in our ring to keep Sam in shape. Gradually, he and I began to bond. He really was a sweet, kind horse but he had a playful side. I began to think of him as a teenage boy. He loved to kick it up in the pasture and was forever chasing me around looking for snacks.

One day my new friend, Claire, invited me to ride with her on the trails. I didn't even know if Sam liked trails or how he would behave. All we had done together was ring work. But at the conclusion of the day more of the classified ad about Sam—now a point of humor with my friends—proved true. Nothing bothered him: Not the big dump trucks barreling down the road on the way to the trail. Not the guns blasting at the nearby gun club we had to pass. Not the steep hills that we gingerly navigated or the rushing streams we forded. He didn't even raise an eyebrow at the deer scattering when we invaded their resting places. He was a born trail horse and he loved it.

So began our new riding regimen. It was heaven in those woods. I never tired of the same pathways because the woods always looked different from winter to spring to summer to fall. Jessica was more and more involved with school, work, friends, and getting ready for college, and I was more involved with Sam. I looked forward to his gentle nicker greeting me in the morning. I enjoyed watching him contentedly grazing in the pasture, and I loved to call out to him and have him call back to me in response. I never tired of the work it took to care for him, preferring to think of it as therapy instead. Life was good.

But things change and they did at our house. The downturn in the economy had an adverse effect on our family business, and my husband had some health issues. My riding was less frequent.

One day another girlfriend's daughter, Morgan, an extremely accomplished equestrian, asked whether I would mind if she started riding Sam. "I think I can make a hunter out of him," she proudly proclaimed. I laughed and said, "If you get him going well enough, we'll take him to a show." With all of our problems, I welcomed the distraction of watching her ride.

In the woods, Sam and I had enjoyed our rather unstructured riding style. I wasn't concentrating on his leads or holding him in a frame. When Morgan worked with him, it was a whole new story. Now I began to understand even more of the ad. As a spectator, I could see what a beautiful mover Sam really was. Morgan worked hard with him all summer. He responded to her careful coaching, and I knew that I had to keep my word and let her take him to a show. We needed to have some fun, and it wasn't important that he place. It would be an adventure. We decided to make a party of it, inviting a slew of family and friends to join us as spectators.

Sometime the week before the show I had a restless night and woke up the next morning clearly remembering my dream. Morgan was riding Sam in a show and in her first class she took the blue ribbon. It was a great dream, but what I really wanted was for Morgan and Sam to have fun and be safe. Ribbons would be a big bonus, particularly because I had acquiesced to letting her take him in Hunter Flat classes instead of the English Pleasure classes for which I felt he was better suited.

The day of the show dawned clear and sunny. The showgrounds were bustling with horses and riders and trainers when we arrived. I hadn't done this horse-show thing in years and I admit I was nervous, especially when I saw one of the notable trainers from my riding days. Morgan's trainer was also there with a group of outstanding riders from her stable, and I could see she was a bit nervous as well. I wanted to caution her not to expect too much. Even with her accomplished skills, Morgan was going up against some pretty fancy horses with extremely experienced riders.

Meanwhile, Sam was acting like our old backyard horse. We unloaded him and tacked him up. He was infinitely more interested in where the hay bag was than in what was going on around him. I began to wonder if we would be able to get him into show mode. I had an additional concern as well. When I went to register him for his classes, I discovered that he and Morgan would be going up against a student of the great trainer from my childhood. At that point I prayed they would just get through the class without missing a lead or breaking stride in front of the judge.

When they were ready, Morgan took Sam to the warm-up ring and confidently put him through his paces. He began to wake up and look like a show horse. I looked into his eyes and saw his interest in his surroundings. Still, I couldn't calm the butterflies in my stomach.

Then it was time. The first flat class in their division was called. I surveyed the competition and my heart sank. These horses all were real hunter types. But then I looked over at Sam and Morgan, and my heart swelled with pride. Sam stood in perfect position, head high and ears forward. Morgan looked calm and confident, and as they entered the ring I thought, *Wow, what a great-looking pair.*

As the class progressed, I was suddenly reliving my dream from the week before. Morgan and Sam executed the commands of the show steward perfectly. Under her careful guidance, the gelding came alive. He moved beautifully, and I could see that the judge had her eyes on him. When the horses lined up at the completion of the class, I didn't have to hear the outcome. The rest of that crazy ad came into my head: "always in the ribbons." I knew the results before the announcer proclaimed, "And the first place and blue ribbon go to Number 271, Morgan Green, riding Sure Ain't Misbehavin!" You could hear the cheering from all over the showgrounds as our entourage let loose with their joy. Well, Sam truly was behavin' that day. He went on to become the champion of his division and, more importantly, the champion of our hearts.

When the thrill of that weekend had died down a bit, I sent an e-mail to the woman who sold him to us. It simply stated, "You sure do know how to write an ad."

Horse Sense

By Lynn Allen

When my father was a boy, he had a mustang mare named Maggie. Actually, she was the family horse, but Dad claimed her as did each of his sisters. Maggie was a tricolored pinto with a firm conviction that people with cowboy aspirations should be able to ride well. She took her job seriously and used any equine trick to teach her riders how to hang on.

The mare was ornery, there's no other word for it. She was hard to catch and impossible to bridle. She bucked, dived under low tree branches, and was a contortionist who could avoid a cactus while depositing her rider in it. She shied at anything and everything, especially if she thought her rider might fall off.

As a baby, Dad's youngest sister, Alice, had contracted encephalitis, which left her severely disabled both mentally and physically. Her right side was stiff and awkward and often experienced spasms, jerking uncontrollably. Alice loved livestock, but her twisted body and strange movements frightened most animals.

Alice wanted to ride like everybody else, but no one, except my father, was willing to risk putting her on Maggie's back, possibly subjecting her to the mare's rotten streak. Dad was the culprit responsible for Alice's first ride on Maggie. To his credit, he always made sure Maggie was tired (and that Grandma wasn't looking) before he lifted Alice into the saddle.

As she grew older, Alice pestered him mercilessly until Dad began to teach her how to care for the horse. Under her older brother's watchful eye, Alice learned to put on the halter and curry the mare. Sometimes Dad took Alice with him to bring in the milk cows, holding her in front of him in the saddle. He was always very careful with Maggie when Alice was aboard and never gave her a chance to pull any of her tricks.

One day, when Alice was about twelve, Dad was late coming home from school. He had promised her a ride on Maggie that day, and so they would have as much time as possible to ride, Alice decided to catch the mare for him. She retrieved the halter from the barn and slowly made her way to the pasture. Nobody could catch Maggie in the pasture, but Alice didn't know that. With considerable effort, she maneuvered around the pasture on her stiff leg, trailing behind the mare, calling and offering treats. Of course, Maggie avoided Alice, but she didn't run away. Alice's full attention was on catching the mare when suddenly she stepped into a hole, lost her balance, and fell. Lying on the ground, more frustrated than hurt, Alice began to cry.

Curious about the commotion, Maggie doubled back to see what all the fuss was about. She approached the crying child and, in a rare gesture of cooperation, stood still and dropped her head slightly, allowing Alice to grab her mane and pull herself back to her feet.

Reaching into her pocket, Alice's twisted fingers curled around the grain cubes and she offered Maggie a handful of treats. Maggie carefully sorted fingers from goodies as Aunt Alice slipped the halter over Maggie's head.

Slowly, Maggie followed the little girl back to the barn. There Alice brushed the mare and cleaned the burrs from her mane and tail by holding the long hairs in her mouth and plucking at the stickers with her good hand.

Alice finished grooming Maggie, and her brother still wasn't home. Fetching the bridle, she clamped the headstall between her chin and chest and pushed the bit toward the mare's mouth. Maggie took the bit, and Alice led her up to the yard, where she sat on the tailgate of the pickup, waiting. Still, there was no sign of her brother.

No one knows when the idea struck or how long Alice spent trying to climb up onto the tailgate and balance there, but once she was standing, she tugged on the reins until Maggie stood beside the pickup. Then she managed to work her crippled leg over Maggie's bare back and clamber aboard.

Both reins were on the left side of the horse's neck, but Alice didn't mind. She was thrilled. She was riding all by herself! Clamping the reins in her teeth and grabbing the mare's mane with her good hand, Alice kicked. Maggie took a step forward. Alice squeezed again, and Maggie took another step . . . and another . . . and another.

Excitement always made Alice's spasms worse, and she was excited when she hollered for somebody to come see her riding. When her mother got to the door, Alice's good hand was clutching the mane and her crippled hand was twisted in the reins, which were still on the left side of Maggie's neck. Alice's crooked leg jerked and twitched against the horse's barrel, and her voice was an excited squeal. Maggie was standing in the middle of the yard, a little tense but perfectly still.

Just about this time, Dad arrived. Alice was rocking back and forth, trying to make Maggie move. Her hand continued to jerk and pull on the reins and her legs were flopping, but the mare refused to step forward. Dad eased up to Maggie and caught the bridle.

Everybody except Alice sighed with relief.

Once Alice had settled down and a family conference was over, Dad rearranged the reins and knotted them so they couldn't fall. Then he took Maggie down to the corral and turned her loose with Alice aboard. The mare carefully carried the excited child around and around. Maggie never spooked, bounced, or even took a fast step, no matter what Alice did on her back.

Soon Alice was riding Maggie whenever the mare wasn't working. They traveled all over the ranch, and Maggie always brought her home, even if Alice didn't know where she was. Eventually, Alice's balance improved enough that she convinced Maggie to trot, but the mare would never lope, no matter how hard Alice hit her with the reins. When Alice fell off, Maggie waited patiently for her to stand up and climb back on.

"It was always amazing," Dad said. "That mare would buck me off and run home or try to dump me in a cactus patch, but she would turn herself inside out to keep Alice from falling off. If I tried to put on my coat when I was riding, she'd do her best to jump out from under me. But even with that spastic leg and Alice holding the reins in her teeth, that ornery ol' mare would take her anywhere."

Today, therapeutic riding centers are common. Hippotherapy is no longer a fringe alternative therapy as more doctors recommend it every year for physically challenged children and adults. These centers carefully choose their equine therapists. Many are retired from showing, racing, or working on a ranch. Some have been rescued from situations where they were treated less than humanely. Once they arrive at a therapeutic riding program, the horses are trained to work with students living with disabilities such as cerebral palsy, muscular dystrophy, autism, Down syndrome, and brain injury. Most horses take to their new jobs quickly, and some people say they come by their therapeutic skills naturally.

Maggie was a natural and she enriched everyone's life, especially Aunt Alice's. She also taught us the secret to what makes hippotherapy work. It can't be found under a microscope or extrapolated from a pile of statistics—what makes it work is the heart of the horse.

The Doctor Is In

By Amelia Gagliano

"Horses are the best therapists," observed a friend who has spent his life around them. Being around horses does seem therapeutic. They are intuitive beings who resonate my mood and usually manage to move me to a better place than where I started. Their fees are reasonable. For a carrot and a good scratch, I can walk out of the barn feeling like I got a lot in return.

My Lipizzan stallion, Oskar, is a particularly talented therapist. He knows just when to challenge me to become a better horse-woman, when to make me laugh, when to put me in my place, and when to console me. He recently demonstrated his capacity to support and care for me at a time of great personal loss.

On Christmas Eve, my husband and I were saddened to say farewell to our oldest cat, Big Otis. He was a creature we had rescued from the street during the years we lived in Saudi Arabia. As we spent Christmas Eve in somber reflection, we realized Big Otis was more to us than just a family pet. He was a symbol of our personal conquest over the challenges of living in the Middle East at a time that was particularly difficult for Westerners: before, during, and after the 9/11 terror attacks. Big Otis represented all the good things we gained from our life over there and—with his considerable girth—he eclipsed much of the bad.

I awoke Christmas Day with the flu. Still in mourning and suffering a low fever, I was determined to uphold our annual tradition of going to the barn to bring Oskar some special treats and a Christmas gift. I also needed to take him to the arena and let him burn off some steam. He hadn't been ridden for a couple days due to my preoccupation with our ailing cat.

I expected the young stallion to be full of excess energy and difficult to handle, but he walked quietly beside me down the driveway to the covered arena. He didn't even offer to reprimand the puckishly playful geldings as we walked by their paddocks. I was starting to wonder if I had another sick animal on my hands. Still, I was grateful that he was so quiet. Between my grief and my flu, I didn't feel sturdy enough to be the sole handler of an enormous, silver horse-shaped balloon. Under my breath, I reminded Oskar that the Macy's Parade is held on Thanksgiving Day, not on Christmas.

We arrived at the arena without incident. Oskar did not run around as expected when I took off his halter. He stood quietly with me until I gave in to my fatigue and walked away from him to take a rest on the bench. He briefly investigated the brand-new royal-blue horse ball I had purchased for his destructive pleasure. Then he began casually sniffing the various piles of manure left by other horses. I found it soothing to watch him as he strolled leisurely about the arena, lifting his lip, softly snuffling the ground, and occasionally leaving a pile of his own for the benefit of the next horse. He concluded his ritual with a good groaning roll in the dirt.

The arena footing is recycled rubber, which is finely crushed and almost black. When Oskar got up, he didn't shake off the dirt the way he usually does. He just stood there with his head down looking at me. Dark, liquid eyes ringed in white peered at me over a somehow-still-noble soot-colored nose. The once silvery-white horse had the vaguely unsettling appearance of a coal miner returning home from work. Amused by this image, I wondered, *Why is he staring at me? What does he want? Is this horse trying to make me laugh?* As a little smile pushed its way to the surface, I couldn't resist giving his new rubber horse toy a good toss.

Any flickering thought I might have had that Oskar was not feeling well was instantly extinguished by his jubilant response to my first pitch. As I hurled the ball across the arena, he launched himself into the air in a manner that would have made his ancestors from the Spanish Riding School of Vienna proud. The sooty, black footing fell from his coat as once again he galloped after the ball with all his might. He tried to come to a halt, grab the ball, and turn for home in one fluid motion. But the maneuver proved to be one that would require some practice. And practice he did: hurling, leaping, galloping, grabbing, turning, trotting, and repeating.

After several minutes of exuberant play, Oskar began to tire of the game. The leap and gallop were reduced to a trot out and a walk back. We continued to play but at half the pace. I was now in better spirits, and Oskar seemed determined to do all he could to keep me there. But I sensed that his enthusiasm was starting to wane. His once purposeful walk modulated to a lazy stroll interrupted by an occasional pause to vigorously flap the now-deflated ball before returning it to his giggling pitcher. One final time, I hurled the ball. As it settled into the black rubber footing with a flabby thump, Oskar turned his head, studied it, and sighed as if to say, *I really don't want to run over there again.* Then he turned and strolled to the nearest corner of the arena, where the red traffic cones are stored. He plucked one from the stack, walked back, and presented it to me. I guess he thought, *Every time I give her that ball, she throws it away. Maybe she will like one of these cones better.* He didn't know why I was sad, but he was determined to make me happy.

Oskar's traffic-cone solution made me laugh until my sides hurt. It felt good to laugh after all those tears. Oskar's dark eyes twinkled in response as he anticipated a treat. Whether he knew it or not, he had paid his respects to the departed by taking care of the person the elderly cat had loved most. My friend was right: horses are the best therapists.

Mercy for My Soul

By *Maureen Joseph*

I climbed aboard my first horse at age six, half petrified and half in wonder at the sheer beauty and grace of these very large creatures. The horses I came in contact with in my younger years were all made of gristle and bone, seemingly with a single-minded determination to assist me in finding another hobby. But I was undaunted by their bucking, biting, and attempts to run away with me. Horses have always been a consistent golden thread woven through the fabric of my life.

Not long ago, at age thirty-five, I sat in my living room with only the flickering light of the television to keep me company. It was close to midnight, and I had stayed up way past my usual bedtime to watch a horse program. I felt like a kid, sitting cross-legged on the floor, my eyes and ears tuned to the set. One of the segments took my breath away. Tears welled as I watched the sheer magnificence of a ballet on horseback, and I knew immediately that dressage was my calling.

Being a Western rider, the conversion was difficult at times, to say the least. I had an old-style, bulldog-type quarter horse who was completely insulted by the thought of direct rein contact, much less the sissy saddle he stoically endured. After two years of trying to make him into something he was not, I decided to sell my best buddy. It was one of the hardest things I ever had to do, but it was done and the horse search was on.

Patience, I kept telling myself, is a virtue. The search for a new equine partner took an immense amount of patience. Combing the papers, looking on the Internet—it all seemed futile as the most suitable horses were out of my price range. I knew I couldn't afford a warmblood and wanted either a thoroughbred or an appendix quarter horse. It was early one Sunday morning when I spied a tiny one-line ad that read, "Registered appendix quarter horse mare, three-years-old, 16 hands, red, $1,000," and gave a phone number. As I wondered whether the mare had three legs or four for that price, I crossed my fingers, called, and arranged to check her out. She was cheap, way too cheap.

There she was with a lovely head, nice clean neck, long legs, and every bit of 16 hands. However, she was painfully thin. Her backbone, ribs, and hips were protruding, and her eyes had no spark. The poor girl was starving. I moved my gaze from her bony frame to her legs, which showed no evidence of injury from the track (where the owner said he bought her). Her feet, however, were in abominable shape. The left front was six inches over-grown and its shoe was dangling. The other three were severely chipped and cracked and missing shoes. While I examined her, she stood quietly, sad eyes pleading me to take her away from her misery. I knew I'd probably be sorry, but I whipped out $500 of my hard-earned cash and handed it to the owner with the under-standing that the balance would be paid the next day.

The following day, I arrived with a roomy trailer borrowed from a friend. The mare loaded quietly, eager to get to the good grassy hay in the manger. Upon arrival at her new home, she settled quickly and even perked up a bit especially when she heard the rattle of feed buckets or the soft fluff of hay coming her way. Her papers revealed that her registered name was Gorgeous Dancer. I certainly hoped she would live up to that. I called her Mercy, a word I would repeat many times, both as her name and in exasperation.

After the slow, careful process of adding much-needed weight to her bones, I put her to work. For six months, I did nothing but groundwork, undoing the trauma from the track. Mercy quickly gained notoriety by flipping over in the cross ties and rearing at the end of a lead rope. Both times, after falling, she must have decided it hurt, because she never repeated the behaviors. To me, the key to her training was to let her think it was all her idea.

Eventually I rode her a few times a week—and by "rode" I mean I spent time on her back and didn't eat dirt. Mercy was coming along. She no longer crashed into the wall of the arena. She had some semblance of control. But she wasn't easy by any means. She was definitely a touch-me-not type of horse.

A year later, after what seemed to me a lifetime, the mare had completed a remarkable transformation. Her coat was a brilliant chestnut, gleaming like a newly minted copper penny. With work, she had put on muscle and was lovely. Eventually she learned to come on to the bit off my leg without cow kicking, and we were finally forming the partnership I had dreamed of.

We entered our first dressage schooling show, and my goal was just to keep her in the ring. We placed! Though it was only a piddling schooling show, I felt like I had just won Olympic gold. I was very proud of Mercy, knowing how hard it was for her to trust.

We were progressing in our training, and I enjoyed every second of it, but at the same time my personal life was deteriorating. There were always money issues, and when my marriage fell apart, it was even more financially devastating. I became a single parent with a horse. Mercy became my touchstone, the one thing I could always count on, and the thought of losing her cracked my heart.

I could no longer afford lessons, boarding, even magazine subscriptions. My daughter and I were lucky if we had enough food and a roof over our heads. I was running at the bare-bones minimum when my sister became a savior, offering to put Mercy on her pasture for a while. I knew that if we were to survive I might have to sell her. I couldn't bear the thought.

I made sure I kept our little house and fed my daughter well. I also decided that ketchup packets and bread weren't all that bad. My precious daughter was just starting high school, but she never whined about what she didn't have or what she wanted. She endured because she felt the same way about Mercy that I did.

Throughout this time, I held on. I would stand next to Mercy in the pasture and pour my troubles into her neck. While she wasn't exactly people friendly, she stood with me silently, sensing my despair and tolerating the tears.

There's an old saying that what doesn't kill you makes you stronger. It also makes you more appreciative, I've found. That hellish time in my life is behind me. Today I'm married to a wonderful man who has the same penchant for the horsey life, and I look out at my own pasture of six horses and can see my copper-penny chestnut mare, now age seventeen.

Mercy is still my touchstone, always catching my eye, the first thing in the morning that I seek. Yes, she still can be cranky and difficult, but we understand each other, and I love that mare. Isn't that what a partnership is about?

The Velvet Touch

By Elizabeth Kaye McCall

As the horse-industry liaison for a popular touring equestrian spectacle, I spent six days a week in the company of some fifty exceptional equine performers. Even so, I sometimes felt that I was on the outside looking in. Immersed as I was in my work, it had been weeks since I'd ridden myself.

The bittersweet irony couldn't have been more poignant. All the benefits my job had to offer were no substitute for time on the back of a horse. But I had no chance to ride, and it was the single hardest thing for me to deal with on tour. Although I usually found a place to ride in each city the show visited, after six weeks in Montreal, I was still horseless and lonely for all that riding brings me.

It was a hot, humid August afternoon, and I was cutting through the long white tent where Cavalia's horses resided, fighting back tears behind the sunglasses I was still wearing. I had just parked my car on the street in front of the towering big top. The broad expanse of the Saint Lawrence River glittering in the distance beneath the sun had seemed surreal as I drove across the Victoria Bridge on my return to the show site from a small-animal clinic in Saint-Lambert on the south shore. The scent of horses brought me back to the present.

Fans hummed inside the stable as I passed the stalls of dozens of stallions who captivated thousands of spectators nightly. As they did most afternoons, many were munching hay or dozing. Along a parallel aisle, grooms escorted some of the quarter horse geldings used for trick riding toward an exit and the grass paddocks that were used for turnout. A lively conversation in French was taking place at the wash racks in the corner as two young women showered a pair of Lusitano horses in preparation for the evening performance. Yet, I barely saw or heard anything as my feet moved automatically through the barn in the direction of my office in the marketing department.

I was still reeling from the discussion I'd had an hour earlier with a veterinarian in Saint Lambert when she asked to keep my cat, Maya, overnight for tests. Intuitively, I knew something was wrong. The results were more than I bargained for. When Maya subsequently was operated on for bladder stones, a biopsy also revealed intestinal lymphoma. The prognosis was utterly dismal. One week post-op at the clinic, the vet had a heartfelt talk with me. If my cat recovered from the surgery enough to come home to my downtown Montreal hotel room, I might, with luck, have a month for a final good-bye with her.

Time stops when I get in the saddle, nothing exists but the moment. I experience an inner balancing and stillness that quiets my mind and emotions. Having no opportunity to ride made the situation with Maya even worse. She was so withdrawn that she didn't seem to recognize me when I visited the clinic. My emotional state was bleak even with the support of several close friends on tour.

It had been more than a week since Maya's operation when I stayed after the evening performance to give a stable tour to Dave Thind. A dressage trainer and clinician, he was then communications director for Equine Canada, which is the Canadian version of the United States Equestrian Federation. As we made our way through Cavalia's stable, we stopped to discuss nearly every horse, and I answered his questions about the show.

Somehow the conversation shifted to my having gone so long without a horse to ride. Incredibly, Dave offered me one of his horses for my remaining time in Montreal. As fate would have it, his chestnut Hanoverian mare, Velvet, was stabled about fifteen minutes from the clinic in Saint Lambert where my cat was hospitalized. After one get-acquainted morning, when Dave's assistant coached me on Velvet, I had carte blanche to ride and basically treat her like my horse. From the first day I was back in the saddle, circumstances began to change.

Serene and clear in my postriding mind-set, I stopped to see Maya at the clinic before heading across the Saint Lawrence River to my work at Cavalia. When she was brought into a private visiting room, I carefully stroked her while she lay on the table, hoping my touch would boost her energy. I also left a shirt to be put in her cage. In contrast to our previous visits, this time she seemed to know me. My buoyant mood from riding remained as I left Maya and drove to the show site.

A day later, feeling a sense of being at home, I walked inside the barn where Velvet was stabled as casually as if she were my own and reconnected with that crucial part of myself that had missed horses for too many weeks. The simple motions of grooming, tacking up, and then riding a horse—even one I barely knew—absorbed me completely. By the time I slipped the cover back over the saddle on its rack in the tack room, I felt a deep acceptance of my cat's fate—whatever it might be.

Later, as I waited in an exam room for Maya to be brought to see me, I knew I'd come to terms with the dear creature's earthly departure if, indeed, this was her time. Yet, soon after I was alone with her, I noticed something had subtly changed about Maya. *She's going to make it!* popped into my mind. How much longer I didn't know, but after two weeks in the clinic, she was doing well enough to be released.

Maya traveled with me from Montreal to Cavalia's next tour stop in Boston and across the entire United States the following year to Los Angeles. Almost three years after that Montreal summer, my one-time rescue cat was still alive. Somehow that miracle will always be linked to Velvet, who helped me reconnect with the transformative experience that riding is for me and filled a gap amid the whirlwind of life on tour.

Rosie

By Audrey Pavia

T he first time I ever touched her was on a damp winter
night. She had just been ridden in her fourth jumping lesson of the day, and the teenage girl who had gotten off had
handed the reins to me at the trainer's request.

The mare stood completely still, but as I reached out to pet her
spotted coat, I could feel the tightness of her neck muscles and
could see the anxiety in her eyes. This horse, named Rosie because
of her rose-colored, mottled coat, had a hard life. She had been a
part of the boarding stable for seven years after coming from a feed-
lot where the killers picked out horses for slaughter.

Though she had been spared the slaughterhouse, her life as a lesson horse was difficult. She worked many hours a day, seven days a
week, jumping fences and bending poles, little children jerking on
her mouth all the while. She had been twitched and hobbled by
stable hands who did not have the patience to talk her through her
profound fear of clippers. She'd been relegated to the smallest,
cheapest paddock in the stable because she was a just lesson horse.

But as I looked at her that night, I saw something more. She
was an appaloosa through and through, from her white sclera to

her mottled muzzle to her striped hooves. Her conformation reminded me of the illustration of the ideal appaloosa I'd seen in breed publications when I was a kid. When I looked at her, I saw royalty.

So I bought her.

In the beginning, she didn't pay much attention to me. When I would come to get her out of her stall, she would just stand there, a dull look in her eye. She didn't acknowledge me in any way as I slipped the halter over her head. I was just one more stranger, one more person who had come to ride her by the hour.

There were times when I wondered what I had done. I'd wanted an appaloosa my whole life. I had waited twenty-five years for this horse. But she didn't seem to be there mentally. She dutifully performed all the tasks asked of her but without emotion. She was like a robot.

Then one day six months later, as she was tied in front of my tack shed, I noticed something different. I had walked away to get something, and out of the corner of my eye I saw her watching me. For the first time, she seemed to notice I was there.

After that, everything began to change. When I came to her stall, her head would go up, her ears would shoot forward. There were times when she even walked toward me as I approached her stall. It wasn't long before I saw a light come on in her eyes. And then one day she put her head against my chest as I stood next to her, and I could feel her give her heart to me.

Our bond seemed to deepen with every passing day. The anxiety she'd had under saddle vanished, and she became quiet and happy. After several months of patient work, she learned not to be afraid of clippers. She'd stand quietly as I trimmed the hairs on her muzzle and bridle path, and then politely ask for a carrot as her expected reward.

Throughout our first two years together, Rosie had bouts of various maladies, little hints of what was to come. While these were isolated incidents, one problem recurred: corneal ulcers. Little did I know that a year later she would lose one eye, then the other to a mysterious ocular infection that baffled my veterinarians and eventually robbed her of her sight.

The day she lost her remaining eye and stood blind in her stall was nearly three years to the day that I had bought her. She'd been through three surgeries and five trips to the hospital, and subsequently had been diagnosed with a serious autoimmune disorder that had contributed to the loss of her eyes. On her last day on earth, I cried and hugged her, knowing that I couldn't ask her to live in a world of darkness filled with prodding needles and terrifying trips to the hospital. She had suffered enough.

Now that she is gone, I have to live without this gentle creature at my side, without hearing her soft nicker and feeling her tender muzzle against my hand. It feels as though my heart went with her on that bleak January day that she left me. People tell me I'll get over it, that time heals all wounds. But no matter what anyone says, I know that there is a part of my heart that will never ever return.

celebrating
the Bond

A Gift Freely Offered

By Ellen Nicholson Walker

At first glance, Dixie was an undistinguished gray, flea-bitten part-Arabian mare. She had spent the first several years of her mature life as a packhorse and then found her way into the lesson string at an Arabian ranch.

When I met her, she was twenty-three years old, though she looked and acted more like eight. She was a notorious puller and runaway. In the mornings when we rode English and sometimes jumped, all the horses wore English bridles and snaffle bits—except Dixie, who sported her Western curb and still took her riders on unintended gallops.

I was seventeen when I spent six weeks at the ranch's summer riding program. I was older than the other girls there but not the star student. I had had my own horses for five years and enough dressage lessons to sit in balance and put a horse on the bit, but several of the other girls were more experienced, athletic, and talented.

Every morning we were assigned a horse and the instructor tried to match each rider with an appropriate mount. The day Dixie's name was posted next to mine I felt pleased that I had been promoted to the ranks of those considered capable of coping with her.

When I mounted, I had an immediate intense feeling of harmony with Dixie—more than with any horse I had ever ridden. I sensed that she was listening to me. She did not pull and she never tried to run off. From my place in the saddle I found that the plain little mare was athletic and fluid in her movements. That night, I begged to ride Dixie every day, and because no one else wanted her, my instructor agreed.

A couple days later, I asked permission to try my rubber-covered snaffle on her. Dixie went quietly and obediently, and for the remaining weeks I rode her in the milder bit. She had a light and sensitive mouth, and I suspected she was grateful for the change from her long-shanked curb.

Toward the end of the summer, we went on an overnight trail ride on the high Wyoming plains. After several hours of riding, we stopped at a small lake to let the horses drink. I was leading Dixie to the edge of the water when I slipped on the muddy rocks and fell directly under her chest, inadvertently yanking the reins as I went down. She was in the process of taking a step, and I was on my back, my stomach directly under her raised hoof. In spite of my weight dangling from her mouth, Dixie somehow balanced on three hooves on the slippery bank until I could scramble out from under her. The potential harm I could have suffered hit me, but Dixie, my rambunctious mare with a reputation for being difficult, seemed unfazed by it all and dipped her head for a drink. It was the moment that defined our summer together. We were a team now, and the acknowledgment of that newly forged trust silently passed between us.

At the end of our last week, the ranch put on a small horse show for the students. There was no audience, and I cannot recall that there were prizes. It was the first time I had ever performed a dressage test. As Dixie finished a smooth, obedient Training Level Test 1, the students who were watching broke into applause.

Since then, I have ridden many other dressage tests in real shows and received my share of awards. I was thrilled when I broke 60 percent at Fourth Level, and I hope to someday ride a creditable Grand Prix. But I don't think any test or award will mean more to me than the applause of those twelve or fifteen girls, several of whom had struggled with Dixie earlier.

As proud as I was of our dressage ride, I knew it was not the result of any great skill on my part. It was a gift freely offered by my horse, my four-legged teacher who showed me that training is something more than reward and punishment. Before that time, I had believed that riding and training were of necessity a contest of wills in which the rider must either dominate or give up authority to the horse. Dixie had clearly demonstrated that she was not by habit submissive, but she could choose to be a willing partner.

I never saw Dixie again after that week and I don't know whether her new behavior carried over to the next group of students, but I will always remember the sense of communication, of awareness and generosity she gave me every time I sat on her back. I have come upon those qualities in a few horses since and have found them to be infallible signs of a horse who will work well with me in the long learning process that is dressage. It is the magic that makes dressage addictive.

Author Ursula Le Guin says in one of her books that a drag-onlord is someone to whom a dragon will consent to talk. As a rider, I would like to be a person with whom a horse will con-sent to carry on a conversation. Sometimes we forget what an honor it is.

My Day to Feed

By *Terri Smith*

The north wind collided with the back of the house and rushed by my bedroom window, sounding angry. I checked the clock with one eye, dimly noting that it was time to get up and wishing it weren't. In the corner, the gas heater glowed warm for a radius of about three feet. Where I was sitting, feet on the floor and out from under the covers, the air was icy.

The old spaniel woke, too, and Java shook herself, then followed me out to the truck and rode with me through the freezing dark to the stable. We pulled into the twenty-four-hour McDonald's at the highway truck stop so I could buy coffee and a biscuit for later. Java sniffed at the warm, buttery smell of the biscuit, but politely pretended no interest.

The engine warmed and the heater began blowing hot air just as we turned down the lane to the stable. As we stopped to open the gate to the barn, the headlights shone across a row of runs behind the stalls. Four heads emerged, ears forward, blankets buckled snugly across the chests below. The horses looked like housewives in robes, peering out their front doors.

They all nickered and nodded at me as I entered the barn. I

had forgotten my gloves. My fingers were numb and I had trouble with the combination lock on the feed-room door. Inside were eight buckets holding two scoops each, except the one for Bravo, the ranch horse who got a half scoop extra, and the one for fat Tot, the pony who got only one scoop, and even that was too much. I carried four pails at a time up each side of the barn. The grain rattled into every trough, and stall by stall, the nickers subsided into contented chewing. Then I was hungry myself and sat down to have the biscuit and coffee, miraculously still warm. My fingers began to recover.

Java came right over so I gave her a piece of biscuit. She licked her chops by way of thanks, lay down on a saddle pad, and watched me climb the ladder into the hayloft—one-handed—without spilling a single drop of coffee. Below, I could still hear the oats disappearing in thoughtful munching and the occasional hoof stomp of pure satisfaction. I tossed each horse two flakes of hay through the square opening above the stall, then went back and gave everyone an extra flake just this once.

I opened the big doors at the end of the loft and gazed beyond the white board fencing to a thousand acres of tree-dotted cattle pasture. The wind had died away with the sunrise and though the air was cold, it had softened. Later I would ride my old hunter Thomas out there, up and down the rain gullies, hopping a few logs. Below me I saw old Java trot out of the barn. She slipped through the fence and zigzagged at an easy jog through the tall, tan grass, searching for rabbits. Soon only her white-tipped tail was visible, tracking through the field like a tiny twinkling periscope at sea.

The horizon was rimmed with bright gold now. Overhead the stars turned milky pale, then vanished. The new sky arched blue, clear. Silence fell around me as the horses nosed the last oats from their troughs and turned their attention to the impressive heaps of hay filling the racks. I continued sitting in the doorway of the loft, letting my legs dangle over the edge, feeling the sun climb, watching the colors emerge from the winter dawn. No one else would be out to ride today. They were all away, and it was Christmas Day—my day to feed.

Royalty

By Samantha Ducloux Waltz

The moment I saw Vida I fell in love, and I was overjoyed at the prospect of owning such a beautiful horse. She was a bit more careful with her heart. She looked down her shapely Arabian nose at me and with her huge brown eyes conveyed the message: *I will go home with you on one condition. You must treat me like a princess.*

I promptly agreed to her terms and wrote a check to her owner, Judy. Vida was a little more expensive than I'd planned, but for royalty I could cut costs elsewhere.

When I explained to Judy that I would need a few days to find a place to board my lovely chestnut mare, Vida seemed to listen intently to the conversation. She flicked her ears, then raised one foreleg and pawed the air as though to say, *Remember, I am a princess. I must live in a castle.* So I found a boarding facility that included forty acres of pasture for grazing, a dozen other horses to be Vida's playmates, woods at the back with trails, and a roomy stall filled with fresh shavings. Vida moved in and for a few weeks seemed to be content as I grew confident leading her.

But as soon as I started riding lessons, she made it clear that her saddle didn't feel quite right. Every time I started to buckle the girth she swung her head around and threatened to nip me. I'd read a lot about saddle fit and I had purchased a nice English saddle from a friend. I'd taken it with me when I went to meet Vida and had tried it on her. Judy and I both thought it fit well. Vida disagreed. Her right shoulder is slightly higher than her left, so I decided the saddle might be a bit snug on her withers. A good pad should solve the problem. "Can you get along with the saddle if we put it on this very expensive pad I just bought?" I asked as I smoothed the pad on her back and then eased on the saddle.

Not if you expect me to bend nicely when we ride, she answered by holding her neck stiffly when I longed her, even at a walk. The situation brought to mind *The Princess and the Pea*, but I'd promised her royal treatment. So I bent a coat hanger to approximate the shape of her back, took some measurements, and borrowed a half dozen saddles from the local tack shop to try. She didn't like any of them. I brought her a half dozen more. She didn't like those either. She tossed her head and sidled away every time I put one on her as if to say, *These are used saddles. Used saddles are for peasants.*

So I offered her several new saddles. They were made of a synthetic material and very light. I thought she'd be pleased. She wasn't. She flattened her ears when I tried them on her. I got the message. Only genuine leather would do.

I looked at the other horses peacefully grazing. Maybe I could trade my princess for the stalwart, blue-eyed appaloosa under the tall pine or the old, gentle buckskin mare. Vida saw my attention wandering, nickered softly, and pushed my shoulder with her nose. I lifted my eyes to hers, and she breathed her warm, horsey breath on my neck. I fell in love all over again, pulled out my credit card, and bought her a saddle of the softest, most supple leather I could find.

She was satisfied, and we continued lessons. I rode her in circles and on diagonals in the arena and followed trails in the woods until we were both comfortable. Finally we ventured out onto the road.

She did well as we rode at a walk along the shoulder, past a field green with spring grass. When she shied at a mailbox, I quickly reined her in. A car passed slowly, and though her walk turned into a jig for a moment, she immediately settled down.

We ambled through a filbert orchard and then crossed the street to a gated dirt road the width of a driveway. My heart sang with excitement. Beyond that gate, open and inviting, lay trails winding down hillsides and across streams. It was real riding, straight out of the dozens of horse books I had inhaled as a child.

I clucked for Vida to move through. She took two steps and stopped. In the pasture to our right three horses were coming to check us out. Was she afraid of them? Four strands of barbed wire separated us from them. My mare danced nervously in place but didn't move forward. Did the row of firs on our left cast shadows that worried her? *You don't really expect me to go down this unfamiliar trail, do you?* her behavior seemed to say.

I did indeed. My patience had limits. I had paid a lot of money for Vida and her saddle. I paid a lot of money every month to keep her in her castle. "You're okay," I said and patted her shoulder as I again clucked to her and pressed harder with my legs. "This is what horses do."

She pinned her ears and didn't budge.

I kicked her hard just behind the girth. Surprised at my firm command, she responded immediately. She scooted backward into the road.

I looked over my shoulder and saw an old blue pickup truck coming toward us. It wasn't slowing, and I realized the driver mistakenly believed I was in control of my horse and could move out of harm's way. Suddenly Vida and I were in a very dangerous situation. I knew my princess would resist taking orders from a commoner, so I did my best to turn into a queen and take charge. Only when I reigned would she respond to my rein.

Because we'd only just begun to establish our relationship as horse and rider, I knew I'd need to give the mare very clear commands. I pulled the reins alternately to get her attention and then I pulled the right rein with enough pressure to bring her nose nearly to the stirrup, turning her in a circle. "Engage the hip to force a change of direction," my instructor had said again and again. A smaller circle would do that, and I kept intense pressure on the outside rein until Vida's circles were very tight. It worked! We were back on the shoulder of the road. I loosened the pressure on the rein, and Vida relaxed her neck, dropped her head, and walked easily through the gate.

We turned onto a narrow, sunlit path, the mare now willing to explore with me. Scrub oak brushed against my legs. A jay scolded in a tree nearby. I leaned forward to stroke Vida's neck. "You can still live in your castle and wear your fancy tack," I reassured her. "Just remember. When I'm around, I outrank you. You are still a princess, but I am now the queen."

Affection and kisses
are always welcomed by
our regal friends.

Horses's eyes are set far apart, allowing them to see objects to the side.

It takes two to tango.

A galloping paint horse showing off his speed.

This beautiful horse is the "mane"attraction on the farm

Don't hate me because I'm beautiful.

Life on the farm, where horse play is always allowed.

Who wouldn't love
a trail-ride?

On Top
of the World

By Melinda Stiles

Sam is twenty-eight and a bit stiff in the joints. I'm fifty-six and can relate. Neither of us allows the hitch in our git-along to stop us from riding. At some level we both know that continuing to ride will allow us to continue to ride.

When we traverse the narrow trail along the mountain behind my house, Sam breathes heavily. I've walked it before and do the same. We pace ourselves for the 1,000-foot ascent. Sam climbs steadily, avoiding rockslides, a tree stump, a washout. Sometimes his back leg slides off the trail, but I don't panic. A horse-experienced friend once told me, "Trust your horse. He will not intentionally put himself in harm's way." I trust Sam unconditionally. He is focused, alert, aware. I learn to be mindful from him.

As we near the ridge, Sam kicks his aching joints into full throttle and bolts to the flat ground. I like to think he's anticipating what awaits us as much as I am, though I know it is easier for him to go faster. I am in awe of his energy at his age. I resolve to remain active.

On top of the ridge, I dismount and pivot in a circle to take in the entire view. The city of Salmon, fifteen miles away, sparkles in the sunlight. The snowy peaks of the Continental Divide loom in the distance. The east fork of Tower Creek babbles silently below on one side of the ridge, the north fork on the other. A wind symphony plays through the ponderosas. Yellow arrowleaf balsamroot flowers sway in time. Bunched at our feet, small round cacti with fuchsia flowers are a surprise. The view from the top of the world is pristine, majestic, serene.

Sam takes in the view, turning slowly side to side. His nostrils flare, delighting in the aromas. A soft nicker escapes his throat. Whenever we find ourselves in this place beyond clocks and deadlines, it feels like Sam appreciates the grandeur as much as I do. Because he is so present in the moment, it is easy for me to be. I feel one with my horse and with nature. My heart is filled to overflowing with gratitude to Sam who makes this experience possible.

Some invisible vibration ripples through us and we know it is time to leave. Fully sated with beauty, we head back down, oblivious to our aches.

Early-Morning Ride

By Jacklyn Lee Lindstrom

Nature's paintbrush splashes streaks of pink and lavender across the eastern sky, heralding the coming dawn. Early-morning air, crisp and cool, tickles my skin as I run from the house to the corral, bridle hung over my arm. Inside the fence, dark silhouettes of horses move back and forth in slow motion. The world is not yet awake.

"Shirlou, Shirlou. Come on over here, gal," I call softly.

A shape disengages from the herd and ambles slowly toward me, her head reaching for the carrot in my outstretched hand. I slip the bridle over Shirlou's ears, lead her out of the corral, grab a handful of mane, and swing up onto her back.

This time is ours: an early-morning ride, a time to be together and greet the beginning of a new day. Two of God's creatures, one two-legged, one four-legged, each with beating heart, throbbing veins, fears, joys, and sorrows. Two beings, separate yet conjoined.

We head out, Shirlou's body soft and warm against my legs as she yields to the commands of the reins and the weight of my body. An obedient creature, she trusts me to guide her safely through the man-made jungle of farm machinery and cars and down the spooky black road with the yellow stripe in the middle. Even though she has been this way many times before, I feel her hesitate, ready to whirl around and run back to her comrades in the corral. But I know her little game and I am ready for it, my legs and hands insisting she point her head toward the woods.

The sun, breaking over the horizon, reflects sparkles of dew on the grass—tiny diamonds, set down while the world was sleeping, to be gathered by the seekers of the dawn.

We head into the woods, dark, quiet, serene. The only sound is the muffled rustling of Shirlou's hooves on the pine-needle trail.

Deep in the cathedral of green, birds dart back and forth like colored arrows, and a feathered chorale sounds their early morning hymn of praise: *Morning has broken* . . . Up ahead, a wary doe watches us, her ears flicking, ever alert. She seems not to fear Shirlou, and we approach close enough to see her nostrils quiver as she detects my scent then bounds into the safety of the woods.

Shirlou has taken charge now, her head swinging from side to side as she steps out, her rocking-chair stride lulling me into dreamy euphoria. Her body is warm against mine, no saddle between us, nothing to disrupt the communication we have with each other. I am the passenger in Shirlou's world now and I willingly submit to her lead. I have learned to trust her, just as she has learned to trust me. She knows these trails better than I. More than once she has found the way through the woods when I thought we were lost.

Shirlou starts to dance and toss her head. We both know what is ahead: the running place, an open meadow with a sea of prairie grass and multicolored wildflowers. It is a place where Shirlou can reach deep into her soul and do what God intended his range creatures to do—run, wild and free, hooves pounding like drums on the tight skin of the Earth, pulsating hypnotically to the music of another time.

I give myself to the one beneath me, descendant of those range creatures who once ran wild and free, perhaps over this same meadow. We race across the field, my hands clutching Shirlou's flowing mane, her heart pounding against my legs clenched tight around her body. The wind rushes past my face, bringing tears to my eyes. My hair whips behind me like a tattered flag. The ground streaks by in hazy patterns as we bound forward in absolute freedom, hooves pounding, pounding on the turf. Shirlou's breath comes in noisy bursts now, and her nostrils flare as she drinks in great gulps of air, the heat from our bodies rising and mingling together.

Too soon it is over. Racing hearts return to normal. Breathing slows as burning lungs are satisfied. The meadow once again becomes a sea of prairie grass with soft-colored wildflowers. And I am at peace.

The sun climbs higher, burning off the early-morning mist, replacing it with harsh light and sharp shadows. It is time to return. We head back through the woods, Shirlou's tail swishing at my legs, brushing at a fly perhaps or at the sweat dripping off her flanks. Birds again warn of our presence and wary animals once more make a safe retreat.

Out of the woods and heading for home, once more I take charge. I guide my obedient servant back over the spooky black road with the yellow stripe, maintaining a careful distance from the tractor, now belching smoke as it idles in the farmyard. Back at the corral I slide off and watch Shirlou roll in the dust, rubbing the itchy sweat off her back. I would like to join her, but I must now return to the world of rush-hour traffic and office cubicles. So I give Shirlou a final pat and hurry to the house for a quick shower, thanking God for once again allowing me the thrill of an early-morning ride.

We're Just Here to Look . . .

By Jennifer Walker

It's all my mother's fault. Everything is her fault. It's her fault that we had horses when I was a kid and it's her fault that I got back into it when I was thirty-two. She started everything.

The problem is the horse gene. You're either born with it or you're not. If you're not, you might like horses, but they won't be a problem. For example, I tried and tried to make my daughter into a horsey girl, but she doesn't have the gene. She likes the idea of horses, but she's scared and doesn't care enough to get over her fear. But if you have the gene, God help you and everyone around you. It's a sickness for which there are no support groups, no twelve-step programs, and no government grants.

I carry the horse gene. I got it from my mother. I've lived, breathed, and slept horses for as long as I can remember. A banner day in my life was when I was nine and my mother said to me, "Jenny, we're going to go look at a horse today." I couldn't believe my ears. Finally, a horse! A horse to love and ride and feed carrots to and brush and clean up after. "We're just going to look," she said. *Right,* I thought.

We went to look at Dolly, a yearling half Arabian, half quarter horse. She had fallen and hurt her shoulder so she was lame, but her seller assured us she would heal in no time. We took her home—"home" being a boarding stable in Cupertino, California. Then what did we do with this lame yearling we'd bought? We loved her and took her for walks and fed her carrots and brushed her and cleaned up after her, but her age and condition prohibited us from riding her.

So off we went to just look at a second horse. By the time ten years or so had passed, we had just looked at about twenty different horses who all came home with us. Several of them were "my bestest friends in the whole wide world," carrying me hither and yon over hill and dale and to many ribbons and plastic trophies and cheap silver trays.

Eventually, little horsey girls grow up and their parents stop footing the bills. Horse gene or no, horses are expensive creatures. When I moved out of the house at the ripe old age of twenty-three, I realized it was time to sell my last horse until I could afford this hobby again. During the years that followed, I dreamed of horses, I read about horses, and I cried over my pathetic lack of horses. I moved to the big city of Sacramento, and soon knew the location of every feed store and tack store. In truth, Sacramento is more a town than a big city, but to a recently expatriated country girl, it seemed like a bustling metropolis. I kept my old saddle and it followed me from house to house, just in case a horse might come by that needed riding. My husband, whom I'd met somewhere along this horseless desert of my life, didn't quite take this seriously. He likes horses well enough, but he isn't cursed with the gene. He doesn't really know what it's like.

The horseless desert disappeared on Thanksgiving Day 2004. We were at my brother's house in Rough and Ready, California, admiring my niece's pony. That was my mom's fault, too. The horse gene somehow skipped my daughter but made its way into my horse-hating brother's daughter. How did that happen? I tried to argue that the girls had been switched at birth, but no one bought it since they're a year apart . . . but I digress.

Jordan has the gene. She's lived, breathed, and slept horses for as long as I can remember. Mom and I heartily encouraged this, giving her horsey toys and books at every opportunity while my horse-hating brother, Martin, groaned and rolled his eyes until we were sure they'd stick. (They didn't, but it was a close call.) Finally, Mom convinced him to let her give Jordan riding lessons for Christmas. From there, his life as he knew it, as he planned it, was over. The next thing we knew, my horse-hating brother was shuttling his daughter to lessons in their new truck and trailer. He was paying the mortgage on a horse property. He was building an arena (with sand and jumps and everything) and owned not one, but two ponies. With two daughters, he never had a chance. Luckily for him, Taylor is a few years younger than Jordan so he has a slight reprieve before things get really bad.

On that fateful November morning, my brother helped me haul myself up onto Shadow, Jordan's eventer. I rode him bareback, at a walk—too chicken to trot—but I was the happiest I'd been in nearly ten years! Right there and then I did a mental budget and decided I could afford a horse again.

My husband's first reaction was to laugh. He thought I was joking. It took a few minutes to convince him that I was, in fact, serious. His reaction then shifted to disbelief. How could I possibly afford a horse?

"They're expensive."

"I'll get a cheap one," I reasoned.

"Where will you keep it?"

"There's a place nearby that boards for $200 per month. I can swing that," I countered.

"What will you do with it?"

"Love it and ride it and feed it carrots and brush it and clean up after it," I explained.

I told him that I had no aspirations of showing "since it's so expensive." (It turned out that I was wrong about that. Oops. I competed in ten shows in 2006 and am making plans for Nationals in 2008.) "It'll be fine," I said, "just wait and see."

I began my search by posting a want ad on the Bay Area Equestrian Network: "Wanted: horse for under $1,000 or free lease. I can afford upkeep but don't have money saved up for a big purchase. Arabian or cross preferred, at least 15 hands. Prefer not green broke." It occurred to me some time later that this probably was not the best method of finding a horse. I sounded a bit like a horse-crazy teenage girl among other things. But I was determined. I would have my horse.

I received several responses to my ad. One was from an Arabian breeder. "I have a horse you might like, $500. Black bay, three years old, green broke. She's 14.3." Not exactly what I had in mind (one out of three ain't bad), but I'm a sucker for bays. I saw a picture of One Hot Lady on the breeder's website and I was sold. I knew from that picture that this was my horse. I made an appointment to visit her and told my husband, "We're just going to look." He apparently didn't know what that meant in my family, so dutifully he came along.

When we arrived and saw the mare, I thought, *Wow, 14.3 was a lot taller when I was a kid.* I was sure I was experiencing the same phenomenon that makes your childhood home look smaller than you remember when you return as an adult. However, we measured the filly later and she was 14 hands, although now she's had a growth spurt and soared to 14.1. Despite her size, or perhaps because of it, she was adorable. It was late December and she had a fuzzy winter coat, her mane, tail, and forelock were long and full, and she had the sweetest eyes. *She's perfect,* I thought. "We're just looking," my husband informed her owner.

The breeder had warned me that the filly would need a tune-up before being ridden so we agreed that I would not ride her that day. We turned her out in the arena so I could see her move, and I melted—this really was my horse. She was so elegant, so graceful. She had such a twinkle in her eye as she galloped and bucked and tossed her head. "She's perfect," I whispered to my husband. "We're just looking," he reminded me.

I wanted to play with her some more, so we put her on a longe line to see how she handled. She was still wound up from her run and continued running and bucking on the longe line until she pulled the rope out of my hand, making an excellent effort at taking my finger with her as she ran to the other end of the arena.

"She's perfect," I said through my teeth, nursing my newly sprained finger. I somehow managed to write a check, much to my husband's surprise and chagrin, and we picked up the filly the next week. It never occurred to me to get a vet check. After all, we were meant to be together, right?

One Hot Lady, aka Molly, has taught me much over the past two years, and all I've suffered has been the aforementioned sprained finger, a few bruises, and one concussion that I currently recall. She's coming along in her training and so am I. My chiropractor and I have become very close.

I think I'm the luckiest girl in the whole world, but my husband just shakes his head. Next week, my instructor and I are going to just look at two thoroughbreds in need of rescue . . . just don't tell my husband!

Must-Know
Info

Must-Know Info
Preventive Care

A good preventive-care regimen needs to stay within the horse's evolutionary framework. Try as best you can to recreate the natural way of life for the domestic horse (with some obvious modifications). With a little creativity and understanding of the basics, you can stay within the framework that will maximize your horse's health.

~~~

Three important foundations for maintaining total health are nutrition, dental care, and hoof care.

Feeding a horse is one of the most daunting and confusing areas of his care. But always consider this: how do horses eat in the wild?

They wander around with their heads down, constantly chewing mostly very fibrous, whole food-plant material. We are lucky horses have adapted as well as they have to being kept in stalls or small paddocks. But what they don't adapt well to is excessive amounts of easy-to-digest carbohydrates with lower levels of coarse fibers provided in feeders rather than on the ground.

Have your horse eat his feed off the ground with his head down. This allows his lower jaw to come forward and maximize the proper tooth contact for chewing and dental health. The better a horse chews his food, the better it digests and he absorbs

the nutrients from it. Feeding head down also minimizes
hay particles and dust getting into the nasal passages, which
could lead to allergies and sinus problems.

Use free-choice supplements. Horses should be presented with both loose mineral salt and loose minerals without salt in separate containers. If you know that your hay or
your area is low in a particular mineral, find an edible source
of it, stick it in a bucket, and hang it up. You'll never lag
behind a deficiency or overdo it by supplying additional sub-
stances that your horse doesn't need.

It might seem odd that I consider teeth a more important
foundation than something like exercise or vaccinations. But
once again we are talking about the most basic foundations of
health. Without them it would be virtually impossible for a horse
to exist.

It isn't feasible for most of us to allow our horses to wander
around grazing acres of grass and brushland. So we keep their
mouths in as close to wild shape as we can by using metal floats
to file the teeth. The average horse should have his teeth done (or
at least thoroughly checked) once a year. The interval for the
adult can vary depending on his anatomy, job, and environment.
Horses younger than five should have checkups twice yearly.

Everyone has heard the adage "no foot, no horse." These
simple words of wisdom are hundreds of years old, but they are
just as true today as they were back then. Neglect of this basic
healthcare foundation can cause serious problems.

To keep your horse's feet healthy, make sure you have a farrier
or hoof caretaker who truly understands the importance of his

role in your animal's health care. When you find that person, take care of him because his visits are going to be a lot less expensive than nerve blocks, x-rays, MRIs, cross-country trips to veterinary schools, and the loss of performance and quality of life for your horse.

Kimberly Henneman, D.V.M., C.V.A., C.V.C., is a graduate of Purdue University School of Veterinary Medicine. She is certified by the International Veterinary Acupuncture Society in veterinary acupuncture and veterinary Chinese herbal medicine, and by the American Veterinary Chiropractic Association in veterinary chiropractic—only the twenty-first such certification in the United States. Dr. Henneman's practice is concentrated exclusively in complementary therapies. She has completed training in both basic and advanced classical veterinary homeopathy and has integrated classical homeopathy for both companion and equine patients into her practice since 1994. In 2006 she traveled to China to study Traditional Chinese and Tibetan Veterinary Medicine and is currently working on a master's degree in Traditional Chinese Veterinary Medicine from the Chi Institute and the Southwest University College of Animal Science and Technology in Sichuan, China. Dr. Henneman can be reached by e-mail at AHOoffice@aol.com.

Mᴜꜱᵵ-Ƙñọⱳ Iñᵮọ
Stable Vices

Stall-bound horses have a tendency to develop strange quirks and habits, which are commonly called stable vices. They include chewing or sucking on wood, cribbing, pacing, stomping, and tipping over water buckets.

~ ~

Although annoying to us, these undesirable behaviors are not usually vices of the horse's character, but are the behavioral consequences of an inadequate living environment. Horses use this behavior to cope with confinement stress, lack of continuous exercise, unnatural diet, and limited social interaction. What people may see as hot digs—living in an individual stall, getting two to three meals a day—is equivalent to a prison cell from the horse's point of view. Stalled horses are locked away from the rest of the herd and unable to free graze and roam as their instincts tell them to do.

Wood chewing, where an individual bites, chews, and sometimes swallows wood, is a serious issue with stalled horses. It can cause colic, internal bleeding, and even death. A nutritional deficiency, the result of a lack of adequate forage in the diet, is the most common culprit behind wood chewing. Salt or mineral deficiencies can also play a role. Providing more roughage in the horse's ration and allowing free access to salt and minerals can reduce this behavior.

Cribbing occurs when a horse latches his mouth onto a horizontal object, like the side of a stall, sucks air through his mouth, and swallows it. Cribbing is often associated with colic, wearing down of the teeth, and weight loss. Horses who are fed large amounts of concentrated grain or who suffer from gastric ulcers are sometimes cribbers. Those with gastric ulcers may crib because this behavior increases salivation, which may relieve gastric discomfort by changing the pH of the stomach.

Circling, weaving, and pacing back and forth are most often associated with separation anxiety. These behaviors may be a way for the horse to cope with increased anxiety caused by seclusion from other horses. Social animals to the core, horses are meant to live in herds.

In situations where equine companionship is not possible, other types of companion animals can help lessen a horse's feelings of seclusion. Chickens, dogs, goats, sheep, and donkeys have been used to provide companionship to lonely horses. Regular exercise and time out of the stall can help to decrease separation-related stress.

Pawing at the ground or at objects is a natural and quite adaptive response of horses in thwarted-goal situations. In a natural environment, pawing is used to accomplish an objective. For instance, when snow is covering forage, pawing uncovers the grass. If ice is forming on a creek, pawing effectively provides access to water.

When a horse's escape is thwarted, he may similarly paw near the perimeter of the area where he is confined. He may dig deep holes in his stall, which have to be refilled constantly. Feeding time is a common motivator for pawing, often because the horse becomes impatient with the time it takes to get his food. Caretakers often inadvertently reward this behavior by bringing the horse his hay first so he won't have reason to paw. Some people walk over to the stall to scold the horse for pawing, which is a reward because it provides attention. Completely ignoring a horse when he paws, often is the best way to get him to stop.

Kicking stall walls is an extremely dangerous behavior, which can both damage the stall and seriously injure the horse. The habit is easily transferred from one horse to many because horses learn from each other. Wall kicking, like pawing, is often linked to feeding time as a horse becomes frustrated. Boredom also is a factor contributing to kicking, and horses seem to enjoy the noise it makes.

Playing a radio in the barn can help lessen boredom and fill the air with something the horse can listen to other than his own back feet hitting the wall. Toys in the stall, like an empty water jug tied to the rafters, can give the horse something else to do. Increased exercise can also help engage his mind. Rubber mats can be placed along the walls in situations where a horse will not stop kicking.

Bored horses may use their noses or hooves to tip or slosh water out of their buckets, creating an annoying and soppy mess in the stall. Similar behavior has been seen in wild horses approaching natural water sources. It seems this behavior is simply the way horses react to water in the wild, although it's not compatible with modern stall limitations.

Certain breeds or individuals with innate high energy, horses who are physically fit, and those on high-energy diets are most prone to problem stall behavior. Stallions and colts faced with thwarted sociosexual goals—such as having mares pass their stalls but being unable to interact with them directly because they are confined—may also show increased problems in the stall. Horses are most likely to develop stall behavioral problems during periods of extreme social separation stress. Many experience these periods during their youth when they are weaned from their mothers.

To help prevent behavior problems, provide your horse with as natural an environment as you can. Remember that turnout, exercise, frequent feedings, and exercise are the best remedies for problem behaviors.

Sue McDonnell, M.S., Ph.D., is a board-certified applied animal behaviorist who is a professor and founding head of the Equine Behavior Program at New Bolton Center, University of Pennsylvania School of Veterinary Medicine. Her work includes clinical, research, and teaching activities focused on horse behavior. Her research interests include several areas within equine physiology, behavior, and welfare. In addition to laboratory and field studies, she maintains a semiferal herd of ponies specifically to study their physiology and behavior under seminatural conditions. Dr. McDonnell is the author of two introductory-level books for horse owners on horse behavior, is coeditor of the most current academic book on horse behavior, *The Domestic Horse*, published by Cambridge University Press, and is author of a book and DVD cataloging behavior of horses under both domestic and natural conditions titled, *The Equid Ethogram*. This practical field guide to understanding horse behavior is available at www.horsebehaviordvd.com.

Must-Know Info
Calming the Spooky Horse

Spookiness is one of the most natural conditions of equine behavior. But what exactly does "spooky" mean? Let's agree that the term refers to a horse being frightened by the sight of an object, a smell, a sound, or a touch.

Every horse is born with the tendency to be frightened of things that are unfamiliar. As he grows, he can become more spooky or less spooky, depending upon his experiences.

The sight of an unfamiliar object—a plastic bag hanging from a tree or someone's jacket casually thrown over a fence—can produce a flight response in many horses, and this natural desire to flee can be very dangerous for a rider or handler. If we are to produce a horse that is safe, we are obliged to help him deal with objects he perceives as a threat to his survival.

For a wild mustang the sight of a helicopter appearing on the horizon and approaching with speed can be an incredibly spooky experience. As the helicopter nears, the mustang hears the rhythmic beating of the prop blades and the roar of a large engine. In his perspective, something is coming from the sky that has no business whatsoever in that position, at least not in the world of untrained horses. Gunfire is also frightening to a horse unfamiliar with the sound. But those who live next to vineyards often graze close to devices that produce gunshot sounds to frighten away birds. I have witnessed horses grazing a few feet from these machines, and once they are conditioned, they don't even stop chewing.

Horses can smell a predator before they see it. The scent of a mountain lion or even year-old lion dung will spook most horses into a frenzy. Virtually every horse on earth becomes spooky when he first encounters the scent of pigs. It is unfamiliar, pungent, and invades the equine olfactory system most dramatically. But horses raised on pig farms are seldom spooked by the smell. When the scent is familiar, they no longer react adversely to it.

Touch can also cause a horse to spook. A person who touches the flank of an untrained mustang is probably going to get kicked. With proper training, the horse can learn to tolerate that same touch in a short time.

A basic rule when it comes to spookiness is that pain and the memory of it increase the intensity while the absence of pain decreases it. The wild horse that sees a helicopter fly over him twice daily soon realizes it is harmless. He receives no pain as a result of the helicopter's presence and so he becomes familiar with it and no longer spooks.

But if the helicopter were to fly over the horse twice a day while someone in it shot him with a BB gun, he would run like the wind, crash through fences, and even cause himself bodily harm far greater than the BB gun could ever do just to avoid the helicopter. It is the source of his fear, not the BB gun. Even if he did not see a helicopter for ten years, I guarantee he would still take flight at the sight of one, BB gun or not.

This is a very important factor to consider when dealing with a spooky horse. Utilizing painful techniques to train him not to spook invariably takes much longer, and he will tend to remember these unpleasant aspects of his training. He will often be intermittently spooky, which is extremely dangerous if a horseman is caught off guard and unprepared to protect himself.

Horses who fear plastic bags, birds, airplanes, trucks, tractors, umbrellas, cattle, sheep, hogs, and even bicycles are brought to me regularly. Of the 8,000 horses I have worked with in public events, approximately 2,000 have been spooky and brought to challenge me. Although I can significantly improve the behavior in the thirty minutes I typically have, it is an insufficient amount of time to resolve the problem. But I can accomplish enough to provide the horse's owner or trainer with a road map for the cure.

Using my Join-Up method, I school the horse so he wants to be with me rather than away from me. I offer him a choice using a system of nonverbal communication that I refer to as the language Equus. My website (www.montyroberts.com) offers resources and clinics to assist horse owners and handlers in becoming more fluent in this language of gestures.

Once a horse wants to be with me, I address the issue of spookiness. I begin to stimulate the fear response by bringing a plastic shopping bag toward him. The item I most rely on to desensitize a spooky horse, the bag is extremely light and can't physically harm him. I also attach several bags to one end of a wooden pole approximately five feet in length.

When I receive relaxation and acceptance from the horse, I take the bag away. Using this method, I can soon swing a massive collection of

plastic bags at him, evoking no flight response. I continue to intro-
duce various objects in an effort to broaden his base of acceptance.

Working in a variety of environments is also key in developing
a horse's overall level of acceptance. Not only should he be famil-
iarized with new objects in the arena, the process should be
employed in all environments: the barn, the pasture or field, on
the trail, in daylight, in darkness.

Utilizing these techniques and recognizing that we are dealing
with the true nature of the horse soon produces an individual not
prone to spook. It is important for the trainer never to blame the
horse for spooking. The horse is not at fault; he just hasn't become
familiar with whatever is causing him to spook. A horseman who
has mastered the basic fundamentals of the Join-Up process can
expect successful results from its use.

Respecting your horse and his right to fear unfamiliar objects
is essential on the journey to overcoming spookiness.

Monty Roberts, the *New York Times* best-selling author of *The Man
Who Listens to Horses*, is an award-winning trainer of championship
horses, Hollywood stuntman, foster dad to forty-seven children, and creator
of the world-renowned and revolutionary equine training technique Join-
Up. Encouraged by Queen Elizabeth II and called upon by trainers the
world over, Roberts, at seventy-three, spreads his message of nonviolence
to incarcerated youth in juvenile detention facilities, gentles wild horses
in front of live audiences, teaches a growing number of students at his
Equestrian Academy in Solvang, California, and advises executives at
Fortune 500 companies. He remains steadfast in his goal to leave the world
a better place than he found it, for horses and for people. Determined to
share his vast knowledge, he offers a free weekly e-mailed question-and-
answer column, "Ask Monty," on his website www.montyroberts.com.

Riders often take their horses up to unfamiliar objects to broaden their range of experiences.

Did I hear a hay fork?

Bucking is usually a defensive technique in the wild.

Horses can usually only see gray, but sometimes they can discern blue or green.

When the fall leaves appear, horses will begin to develop their winter coat.

Boots and leg wraps on this dapple help protect him from clipping his front legs with his back hooves at fast speeds.

Ready for a ride.

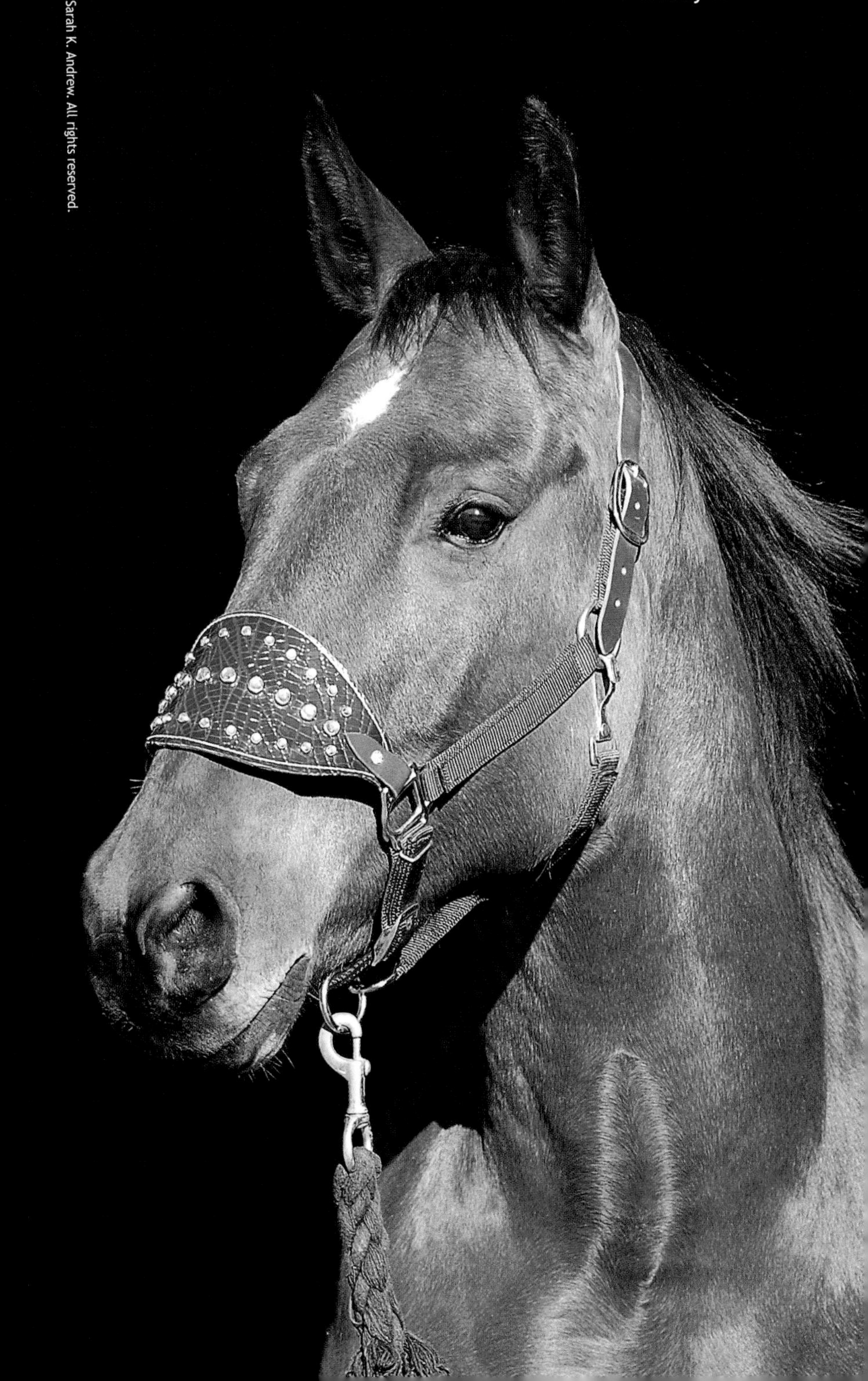

The grass really is greener over here.

Must-Know Info
Healthy Feeding Basics

*Nutrition is one of the most important aspects of horsekeeping.
Horses evolved to be virtual eating machines, and what you feed
them—and how often—is crucial. Keeping your horse healthy and at
the right weight isn't hard if you know the basics.*

For starters, provide your horse with as much turnout as possible. Give him small meals in between regular feedings so you
can add supplements or more calories to his diet.

Provide your horse with a consistent diet. This will help to
maintain the health of the beneficial bacterial flora living in his
intestinal tract. Make sure he has hay or pasture at all times, too.
You'll keep his digestive system working that way.

When determining your horse's diet, remember that all horses
(depending on their calorie requirements) need at least 1.5 to 3 percent of their body weight in forage—hay or pasture—each day. They
also need clean water, free of algae and bird droppings. Water should
be warmed in the winter to at least 50°F, and it should always be
convenient. Horses drink eight to twelve gallons of water per day.

Horses also need salt. Provide your horse with a plain white salt
lick. If he ignores it, add 1–2 tablespoons of table salt to his feed
each day.

Horses who require more energy for their work can benefit from concentrated feed. These are foodstuffs that are relatively low in fiber but high in calories from carbohydrates, protein, or fat. Cereal grains (oats, corn, barley, and more), soybean meal, seeds and seed meals, and fats are all concentrated feeds.

You can also offer more calories than hay or pasture provides without the high carbohydrate levels of concentrates. Digestible fibrous feeds include beet pulp and bran. Bran has more phosphorus than calcium, so be sure to obtain a product that has added calcium to correct this ratio.

In addition to grass hay, you can offer your horse legumes. The most popular legume for horses is alfalfa, which comes as hay, cubes, or pellets. When fed with grass hay or pasture, alfalfa improves protein quality, which is necessary to produce muscle, skin, hooves, hair, bone, tendons, blood proteins, antibodies, enzymes, and more.

You may also want to consider giving your horse supplements to fill nutritional gaps, assist with particular medical disorders, and aid in optimizing health.

The most basic approach for keeping your horse healthy is to realize that all horses are "trickle feeders." This means they require forage at all times. Horses in their natural setting graze virtually all day. This is a very important concept to understand. The equine digestive system needs forage in it most of the time to avoid problems. Horses' stomachs, unlike our own, produce acid continually. If a horse goes for hours without anything to graze, the excess acid in his stomach can produce ulcers as well as diarrhea, behavioral problems (the result of pain), and even colic. Chewing produces saliva, which acts as a natural antacid. A horse who has no hay or pasture will chew on anything available to produce saliva. Furthermore, not eating is stressful for a horse and results in the secretion of stress-related hormones that promote fat storage. So putting an overweight horse on a diet by reducing the hay he consumes actually works in reverse—it promotes weight gain.

A horse who has all the hay he can eat will eat less. Once he sees that he can walk away and the hay will still be there, he will self-regulate his intake and maintain a healthy weight.

Juliet M. Getty, Ph.D., with Getty Equine Nutrition, is an equine nutritionist in private practice in Bayfield, Colorado. She earned her master of science degree in animal nutrition at the University of Florida, and completed her doctoral course work in animal nutrition at the University of Georgia. Dr. Getty continued her studies at the University of North Texas, where she earned her doctorate. Visit the Getty Equine Nutrition website at www.gettyequinenutrition.com.

```
┌─────────────────────────────────────┐
│  ┌───────────────────────────────┐  │
│  │                               │  │
│  │       Must-Know Info          │  │
│  │     Happy Feet: Hoof-Care     │  │
│  │         Essentials            │  │
│  │                               │  │
│  └───────────────────────────────┘  │
└─────────────────────────────────────┘
```

Without his hooves in healthy condition, a horse quite literally doesn't have a leg to stand on. That's why few aspects of horse care are as critical as proper hoof maintenance.

Proper care starts with daily picking and cleaning of the hooves to prevent painful infections of the frog (the soft area in the middle) and to catch little problems before they become big ones. Preventive care also includes professional trimming of the hooves every four to six weeks, no matter if a horse has shoes or not. Done correctly, these routine trims should not make the horse tender-footed. They should be minor adjustments that maintain his balance and comfortable movement.

When horses suffer hoof problems, genetics are commonly blamed but are rarely the true culprit. It's more likely that diet, environment, and the horse's general health factor into the health of his hooves. Hoof issues often signify larger health or dietary problems that can rob vitality from every aspect of the horse's being.

Horses have dietary needs that are very difficult to fulfill in captivity. Starvation periods between meals can be very harmful to the horse. He needs to almost constantly nibble on high-fiber, low-carbohydrate forage. But cultivated grasses, grains, and even some hays generally provide far more carbohydrates and sugars than nature intended. To counteract this, begin by maximizing the amount of hay in your horse's diet and minimize the green grass and grains. Even then, the domestic horse usually suffers from constant carbohydrate overload that must be countered with high levels of exercise.

As they are for people, high-sugar diets ultimately cause a variety of serious health problems for horses. The hooves will usually show the first warning sign that dietary adjustments are needed. A high-sugar diet will generally place a series of ripples on the hoof wall and weaken the attachment of hoof to horse. The hoof walls will typically be disconnected or flared, and lameness is common.

Another factor that can rob health, performance, strength, endurance, and longevity from the horse is the imbalance of vitamins and/or minerals. Again, these problems can often be noticed first in the hooves before they affect the whole horse. Disconnected or weak hoof walls, stubborn wall cracks, and thin, weak soles or frogs should alert you to these problems. An over-the-counter loose mineral supplement often helps, but sometimes analysis of the forage and careful professional mineral balancing may be needed.

Environment is a key factor as well. A soft, wet, or unsanitary living environment will generally produce a weak, vulnerable hoof. Horses should be kept in a herd and allowed plenty of room to roam over firm, variable terrain.

When caring for a barefoot horse, it's important to remember to use professionally fitted, modern hoof boots for protection while riding if his living environment is not as harsh as the riding environment or his workload exceeds the current health and capabilities of his hooves.

It is critical that horse owners educate themselves about hooves and their care, and follow the advice of their veterinarian and farrier. The same knowledge that grows a healthy hoof produces the healthiest horse as well.

Pete Ramey is a natural hoof-care practitioner and author of *Making Natural Hoof Care Work for You* as well as numerous articles on the subject of hoof care. He conducts clinics around the country designed to provide a high level of hoof-rehabilitation knowledge and understanding to vets and farriers. His website is www.hoofrehab.com.

Must-Know Info
Finding the Perfect
Boarding Stable

For owners who cannot keep their horses on their property, a boarding stable is a suitable option. As you begin to consider the facilities in your locale, it is helpful to first decide what is most important to you and your horse. Is it expert care, where the equine residents are supplied with high-quality hay and fresh water and turned out daily? Is it the expert training your horse will receive as he works with a skilled and experienced professional who has proven himself in competition? Are you looking for an impressive facility with both indoor and outdoor arenas, round pens, wash racks, and well-appointed stalls? How about proximity to good riding trails? How strongly do you feel about a friendly atmosphere?

Ideally, the stable you choose will have all of these attributes, although your budget may force you to make some concessions. The more a stable has to offer, the greater the price of board. Monthly fees can run anywhere from $150 for daily feeding and stall cleaning to $800 for a facility with fancy barns and a lot of arenas, turnout areas, and trails.

Once you've determined what is important to you, prioritize your requirements. Now, with this list in hand, you are ready to go out and find your dream barn.

Check the phone book, regional horse publications, and the Internet, but don't discount word of mouth. Ask others with horses where they board and why. Fellow riders can paint a truer picture of a boarding facility than any advertisement ever will.

Once you've narrowed your selection to places with the features you're looking for, call to set up appointments and allow each stable to roll out its welcome mat. A surprise visit will give you a perspective of how the stable usually operates. However, if you come at cleaning time or at the peak of the lesson schedule, things may be a little chaotic—and provide an unfair representation of the way the stable is run. Besides, you can truly gauge a barn's eagerness to welcome you by how prepared management is for your visit.

As you tour, look for signs that the horses are happy. Do they come forward to greet you as you walk by? A barn full of friendly horses sure beats a facility full of sullen or angry ones.

And what about the people providing the care? Is the person who is giving your tour friendly and receptive to your questions? Does she ask about your needs and about your riding abilities and goals? This conversation is an interview of sorts for both of you. Just as it is important for you to learn about the boarding stable, it is equally important for those running the facility to get a feel for you and your needs.

Boarding stables are businesses, and you want to make sure the facility you are considering is run as one. Ask to see the boarding agreement you'll be signing as well as a list of barn rules to make sure the facility is professionally run.

If everything looks good, go meet some of the other boarders.

You will get a sense of the people with whom you'll be spending time as well as have an opportunity to ask more questions about what really goes on.

Good boarding stables are not necessarily the fanciest. The best facilities balance the needs of the horses with the needs of the clients. This is, after all, where you come to escape, so it pays to make sure your choice is an oasis for both you and your horse.

Jennifer Rowan owns Beardsley Publishing, a family business started in 1962. She took over in 1991, and in 2000 started *Stable Management*, a trade magazine for horse professionals. The idea to publish *Stable Management* grew from Rowan's experience running a thirty-stall training and boarding facility with her husband in Connecticut. For more information, visit www.stable-management.com.

Must-Know Info
Tips for Trailering and Travel

A hundred years ago, horses were the Chevy Malibus, Ford F-150 pickups, and John Deere tractors of the day. They transported people, hauled loads, and worked the soil.

It's one thing to go from wild animal to domesticated beast of burden under your own power with your feet solidly on the ground. But it's quite another to be transported from Point A to Point B inside an aluminum cave with the ground speeding by somewhere beneath your feet at 70 miles per hour. It shouldn't come as any surprise then that trailering can be more than a little stressful for some horses.

Why do horses hate riding in trailers? Imagine being trapped inside a dark, swerving, bouncy, noisy, sometimes hot, sometimes cold box, and not knowing where you are going. A horse is programmed for forward movement and he can become extremely anxious when he perceives that he is trapped inside a small space and can escape only by backing out. That's the reason some horses put up such a fuss when it's time to get into a trailer.

You can make a trip in a trailer less scary and possibly even enjoyable for your horse by following these guidelines:

- Give him hay to munch while he's traveling. Don't offer sweet feed, however. The excess energy he may get from it could cause him to feel wound up and anxious.
- Open the trailer windows or slats so he'll have a better view.
- Maximize his travel space. A partition that does not go all the way to the floor allows a horse to plant his feet as widely as possible for balance.
- Protect his leg with wraps, especially those made specifically for travel. He'll be less likely to injure himself if he loses his balance and scrambles.
- Fit him with a mesh fly mask to protect his eyes from flying debris.
- Drive carefully and take it easy around corners.

Preparing your horse to travel well in advance of any trip—short or long—also will help to ease the anxiety he may feel so he's able to take traveling in stride. Here are several suggestions for making loading and unloading routine:

- Accustom a reluctant loader to the trailer long before you're scheduled to depart. Spend several sessions loading him into the trailer and immediately taking him off. Repeat several times until he realizes that once he goes in, he gets to come back out.
- If your trailer has a drop ramp, first walk your horse over a strong piece of plywood that you've placed on the ground to get him used to the sensation of walking on an unfamiliar surface. Then try leading him up the trailer ramp.

- Practice backing your horse out of his stall many times before asking him to back out of a trailer.

- Train your horse to listen, trust, and respond to commands such as "easy," "step up," and "back."

- If you're having difficulty getting your horse to back out of a straight-load trailer, consider getting a slant-load model that will make it possible for him to turn around inside and then be led out.

- Before loading your horse into any trailer, open the partition as widely as possible as well as all doors and windows in the front. You'll increase the amount of light inside the trailer and make it more inviting.

Long-Distance Shipping

Shipping a horse over many miles can be especially stressful, and some equine travelers develop respiratory illnesses on the heels of a long-distance trip. Confinement—standing on a moving platform for hours on end—and the horse's inability to lower his head to ground level so his respiratory tract may drain can be contributing factors. So is poor ventilation that may leave him breathing noxious roadway fumes or air that smells of urine and is contaminated with bacteria from manure. A horse also may experience illness-causing stress if he is not socially compatible with the other equine travelers with whom he's sharing the trailer.

Dealing with health challenges before, during, and after a long-distance trip can help to prevent a horse from developing the condition known as shipping fever. Here are several guidelines:

- At least ten days prior to shipping, have your horse receive the inoculations recommended by your veterinarian. If your horse is treated with joint injections and other therapies that involve the administration of corticosteroids, have your veterinarian give them at least seven—preferably fourteen—days before shipping.

- Make sure your horse is completely healthy at least one week prior to shipping. If he has been ill recently, blood work performed by your veterinarian will verify whether his health has returned to normal.

- Colic can also be a concern during shipping. Talk to your veterinarian about administering a laxative before you leave on your trip. A bran mash with up to one pint of mineral oil can be fed for two to four meals prior to shipping.

- To ensure that your horse maintains good hydration—which can prevent colic—electrolytes can be administered in his feed two to three days before shipping. Although they were commonly dispensed in past years to help prevent illness, antibacterial and anti-inflammatory medications are usually not recommended prior to departure.

Good management during a long trip also is important. If you are covering many miles, consider that a large shipping van tends to be less stressful for a horse than a small trailer. Unnecessary movement is minimized and ventilation is optimal in a larger van.

Although it may be tempting to feed an unlimited amount of hay while you're traveling, offer only as much as you would normally provide at home. Monitor your horse's manure pro-duction during the trip to make sure he is passing all his food. It's also worth noting his water intake and urine production.

If possible, allow a break at the halfway point of your trip to give your horse a rest. Use this time to take his temperature and make sure he's feeling okay. Hand-graze him or turn him out if possible to allow him to lower his head so that any mucus that has accumulated in his trachea may drain.

If your horse has a fever, won't eat, or appears depressed during the trip, consult your veterinarian immediately. And it is also a good idea to alert a veterinarian at your destination to be ready to examine your horse if he arrives sick.

Take your horse's temperature just as soon as you arrive. A normal temperature (plus or minus one degree) for a mare is 100 degrees F (37.8 degrees C) and 99.7 degrees F (37.6 degrees C) for a stallion.

Horses, like all animals, will exhibit a rise in temperature if they are nervous and if the ambient temperature is high (e.g. trailering in 110 degree weather). He may have a significant fever upon arrival which is not uncommon. If he has an appetite and shows no sign of depression, you can wait an hour or two to recheck his temperature before calling a vet. If your horse's temperature returns to normal and he seems to be his old self, there's no need for veterinary inter-vention. Just monitor his temperature for the next couple days.

However, immediate veterinary intervention is especially important if his temperature is significantly elevated and he is depressed and not eating. And, if your horse's temperature stays more than two degrees above normal, give your vet a call.

Mark Baus, D.V.M., is president of Fairfield Equine Associates in Newtown, Connecticut. Dr. Baus has spoken at the local and national level on a wide range of equine-related topics, including issues of practice management. He has contributed to numerous publications, sharing advice on equine health and managing an equine practice. In years past, Dr. Baus enjoyed horse showing and foxhunting. He received his colors with the Fairfield County Hounds in 1989.

Must-Know Info
Equine Posture

Gravity. It's not just a good idea. It's the law! This goes for horses and dogs as well as for people. Pretty much all activity on Earth is influenced by gravity, and the forces generated by gravity are the primary source of most athletic injury. However, running and jumping do not cause most injuries—as you might think. Instead, they originate from how a person or animal uses its body while standing. This is especially critical for horses because they spend twenty to twenty-two hours a day standing: standing and eating, standing and sleeping, or just plain standing.

What goes into posture?

Do you ever think about what it takes to stand up? You have to organize your legs joint by joint, engage your spine, support your head, and keep the whole apparatus from falling over. All these tasks are done unconsciously by postural control centers in the brain that process information about the body's position in space. The nerves that receive information and take it to the central nervous system are called afferent nerves; proprioceptors are a special class of these nerves.

Proprioceptors tell the brain where different parts of the body are: feet on the ground, head in the air, how much each joint is bent, and more. The most important information needed to generate posture comes from the position of the head and upper neck, the contact between the feet and the ground surface, and the position of the temporomandibular joint (TMJ)—also known as the jaw joint. These areas are very rich in proprioceptors and the information they transmit to the postural control centers generates the correct standing posture needed to keep an animal upright.

Normal and compensatory posture

When a horse stands normally on level ground all four cannon bones are perpendicular to the ground like the legs on a table (see photo page 197). The equine anatomy is adapted so this posture is the most energy efficient. Any other posture is a compensatory posture, which takes more muscular energy to maintain and puts strain on tendons and ligaments.

There are normal, appropriate compensatory postures, such as when a horse stands uphill or one leg is injured and he shifts his weight to the other three. More often, we see abnormal compensatory postures, which are created when distorted information from the neck, feet, or TMJ is sent to the postural control centers.

What causes compensatory posture?

Though they are the same genetically and physiologically, most domestic horses live in a world that is quite different from that of the wild horse. Instead of wandering the range all day grazing, our horses stand on wood chips in a ten-foot by twelve-foot room, get a couple meals of high-calorie food, and exercise—if they are lucky—one to two hours a day. They have restraints (halters, bridles, cross ties) on their upper necks. They depend on a farrier to trim and sometimes put shoes on their feet, and once a year, a veterinarian or an equine dental technician files down their teeth.

All these changes in the natural ecology of the horse are part of the compromise of living among people. We do the best we can for our horses, but sometimes it isn't quite good enough. Inadequate exercise and lack of appropriate ground surface change a horse's hoof growth and shape. Farriers do the same, sometimes making the hooves better and more functional, sometimes inadvertently making them worse. Eating small amounts of grain rather than large amounts of hay or forage not only alters horses' digestion, but changes the way they grind their teeth, affecting the position of the TMJ. Getting shanked or pulling against cross ties can damage the delicate muscles of the poll. All these things contribute to abnormal posture by distorting the neural signals that inform the brain about the body's position in relation to gravity.

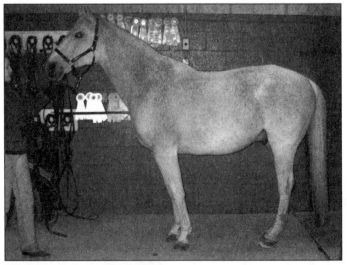

This horse displays normal posture.

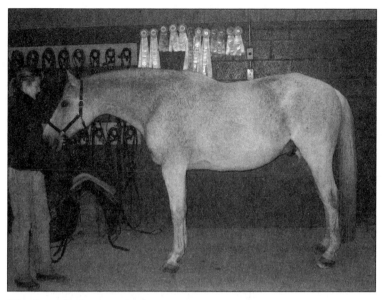

This horse displays compensatory posture.

How does this work?

One of the most common causes of abnormal compensatory posture is imbalanced hooves, especially long toes. Excessive toe length stretches the flexor tendons and puts pressure on the heel of the foot. The same thing happens when a horse stands facing uphill. Long toes confuse the brain—it thinks the body is on a hill—so the horse puts his front legs back in relation to his body. But since he is actually standing on level ground, he must use his hind end to counterbalance. Otherwise, if he leans forward, he will fall on his nose.

The result is the common compensatory posture we call "goat on a rock," where both front and hind legs are camped in (see photo above). In this posture, the horse's weight is pitched to the rear, so that he stands heavier on his hind end than his front. Normally, a horse carries

55 percent of his weight in the front and 45 percent in the rear.

Chronic compensatory posture of this type can be the primary initiating cause of back soreness and hind-limb lameness as well as heel pain (sometimes called navicular syndrome). Back pain occurs because the long muscles of the back are overworked to hold the body in an abnormal position.

Hind-limb lameness can result from the horse carrying an inappropriate amount of weight in the hind end, overloading the hock and stifle joints and causing premature arthritis. Heel pain can develop from always rocking back on the heel of the foot, which crushes the digital cushion and damages the navicular bone. Amazingly, many of these syndromes can improve when the horse starts standing up straight. The same postural abnormalities can also be caused by problems with dental occlusion or injury to the poll.

How can I recognize abnormal foot balance?

Take a ruler and measure the width of each hoof's frog at its widest part, which should be the weight-bearing portion of the heel (the end of the shoe). In a horse with normal posture, the front frogs will be wider than the hind frogs. Now take your ruler and find the widest part of the entire hoof. A healthy hoof tends to be round, not oval or spade-shaped.

The widest part of the hoof is the center from front to back. A horse's heel support should be at the widest part of the frog. So if the heel to centerline measure is one-half the length of the foot, there should be an equal distance from the center to the breakover point on the toe—the last part of the foot to leave the ground. If your horse has more foot in front of the centerline than behind it, his toes are too long.

Ask your farrier to bring the heels back to the widest part of the frog and put the breakover the same distance the heels are to the center of the foot (also called the bridge). This will balance the foot from front to back so the horse can bear weight evenly. If your horse has had long toes for some time, it may take a few days to a few weeks for him to adjust to his new trim. Hang in there. The improvement will be worth it.

What else can I do to improve my horse's posture and health?

Good dental equilibration is essential for the horse, whether he's an elite athlete or a pleasure mount. Find a veterinarian who specializes in dentistry—preferably one certified by the International Association of Equine Dentistry—and make sure he equilibrates both front teeth (incisors) and cheek teeth (molars). Most horses should have a thorough oral exam once a year. A horse who is sensitive at the poll, has a stiff neck, or is head shy may benefit from someone with specialty training in veterinary manipulative therapy—either chiropractic or physical therapy.

Once your horse can generate and maintain a normal standing posture, he should be able to heal most body strains caused by poor hoof balance, dental malocclusion, or poll dysfunction. Sometimes a horse who has had abnormal posture for a long time may need some help reprogramming his system. You can find a practitioner trained in Postural Rehabilitation at www.posturalrehabvets.com.

Remember, a horse will be healthiest and happiest when he can live like his wild cousins. Give him lots of turnout and allow him to go barefoot when possible. If your horse lives in a stall most of the time, make the floor as level as you can so he doesn't have to stand on peaks and valleys all day long.

Domestic horses live the good life in many ways—free food, safety from predators, shelter from the wind and rain. We can go a long way to mitigate the disadvantages of living among people once we recognize the problems and their sources.

Karen Gellman, D.V.M., Ph.D., is a graduate of Cornell College of Veterinary Medicine, and has a doctorate from Cornell in animal locomotion biomechanics. She has advanced training and certification in veterinary acupuncture and veterinary chiropractic. She has also studied physical-therapy techniques with some of the leading equine physiotherapists in England and Canada. Dr. Gellman teaches internationally about posture, complementary therapies, and biomechanics; her students are horsemen, veterinarians, and physical therapists. She also is involved with both clinical and basic science research about posture in horses, dogs, and people. Learn about her work and upcoming events at www.equine sportsmed.com, or find a Postural Rehabilitation practitioner at www. posturalrehabvets.com.

Musʄ-Kñọẅ Iñʄọ
When to Call the Vet

Something's not right. It's feeding time and one mare is standing with her back turned toward the other horses hungrily munching alfalfa. Normally the mare is enthusiastic about eating, but today she seems completely uninterested. Is she just not hungry or could she be sick? Does this situation call for a veterinarian's visit or is she exhibiting normal horse behavior?

Many times owners feel afraid to call the vet because they don't know if a horse's behavior constitutes an emergency. Most people know that a horse who has a gushing wound or cannot stand requires immediate medical attention. Yet many times horses show only subtle signs that something is wrong. They don't display overt symptoms, making many owners hesitant to call the vet.

Here are some easy-to-follow guidelines to help you know whether a call to the vet is warranted. Consider these four levels of concern when you are confronted with a sick or injured horse. They will help you understand the urgency of his symptoms and the overall emergency level of his situation. The four levels of medical urgency are:

Level 1—Critical: immediately call your veterinarian

Level 2—Urgent: contact your veterinarian that day or the following morning

Level 3—Elective: request veterinary attention on a routine scheduled basis

Level 4—Regular preventive care

Level 1—Critical

Level 1 conditions demand immediate professional care and can include:

- nonweight-bearing lameness, such as a fracture
- sudden or severe inability to breathe normally; rapid, distressed, asthmaticlike breathing or an obviously obstructed upper airway
- persistent bleeding from an orifice or wound
- severe or persistent colicky behavior—repeated rolling, pawing, kicking at belly; the progressive course and high risk of many colic cases makes it very important to call for veterinary assistance as soon as signs are noticed
- sudden onset of severe neurological dysfunction, such as staggering, incoordination, or profound behavior change
- sudden onset of blindness, obvious ocular trauma, or unwillingness to open the eyelids
- any mare who takes longer than 30 minutes to complete her second stage of labor while giving birth
- acute laminitis, demonstrated by a stretched-out stance,

severe lameness, or the unwillingness to stand (only if there is no prior history of laminitis or the horse has a sudden, severe recurrent episode)

- any trauma at or near a vital structure, including the eyes, genitals, orthopedic components (joints, tendons, ligaments, synovial compartments), and major nerves and vessels (for instance, those located in the throatlatch)

- any trauma in need of immediate attention for cosmetic reasons, such as a torn ear tip

- high fever—greater than 104°F

- heatstroke, demonstrated as lack of coordination, inability to sweat, high temperature

Level 2—Urgent

Level 2 conditions will need prompt attention, but can usually be managed well with prescribed first aid until a veterinarian can arrive. Examples include:

- low-grade fever—101–104° F

- sudden onset of weight-bearing lameness

- trauma that is superficial, away from vital structures, not compromising normal vital function, and not in need of immediate attention for cosmetic reasons

- signs of less-severe colic—poor appetite, dullness, diminished fecal passage

- flare-up of chronic laminitis (slight to moderate lameness)

- flare-up of chronic inflammatory respiratory disease (also known as chronic obstructive pulmonary disease, an immune-mediated disease of horses with many similarities to chronic bronchitis and asthma in people; characterized by rapid respiratory rate with excessive effort to expire air from the lungs)

Level 3—Elective

Level 3 conditions can persist without deterioration until your veterinarian can arrive or prescribe on a scheduled basis. Examples include:

- intermittent and slight lameness
- persistent dermatitis (flakey, scabby skin)
- intermittent and slight ocular discharge with no sign of pain or poor vision
- reduced appetite with no other symptoms
- slight difficulty chewing
- slight nasal discharge with no fever or labored breathing

Level 4—Preventive

Level 4 care includes routinely scheduled physical examinations, immunizations, parasite control, dental care, nutritional consultation, and general husbandry.

To minimize the risk of emergency calls and keep your horse healthy and active, adopt a proactive preventive approach to managing his overall health and welfare by having a structured wellness program in place.

Know the Vital Signs

Learning to take your horse's vital signs can have significant benefits for monitoring his health. You will be able to see if his readings are within the healthy range for most horses. You will also determine what is normal for your horse and more readily detect subtle changes in his health.

An easy way to take a horse's pulse is to feel for the artery right underneath his jawbone; the site is similar to the area on a person's neck where a pulse can be taken. Count the number of pumps per minute to the heartbeat. In a healthy horse the range should be 29–40 beats per minute.

To take a horse's respiratory rate, count the number of times per minute his gut expands as he inhales. The normal range for a healthy horse is 10–20 breaths per minute.

The average temperature of a horse is 98.5–100.5°F. Monitoring your horse's temperature is a good way to track how he's feeling. Buy a special equine rectal thermometer. Many have a looped end where a string or thin nylon rope can be tied. The other end should have a clip that can be attached to the tail. This is to keep the thermometer from becoming lost or lodged in the horse. Lubricate the thermometer before inserting.

Gum color can also indicate changes in a horse's health. The normal gum color is light pink, and the average capillary refill time for a healthy horse is two seconds. This measure is obtained by pressing a finger to the gum until the spot turns white, then counting the seconds that pass until the gum recolors.

Recommended First-Aid Kit Supplies

- thermometer (a digital one works well)
- stethoscope
- scissors
- adhesive tape
- duct tape
- hemostats
- leg wraps
- soap
- flashlight
- clippers
- phone numbers
- latex gloves

- antiseptics (chlorhexidine, Betadine Solution)
- wound dressing
- hoof pick and knife
- phenylbutazone (bute)
- bottles of sterile saline
- PVC pipe for splinting
- sterile bandage materials: roll cotton, gauze pads, clingy plastic wrap
- sheet cotton
- Elastikon elastic tape
- Vetrap bandaging tape

Harry Werner, D.V.M., has practiced equine medicine and surgery since his 1974 graduation from the University of Pennsylvania School of Veterinary Medicine. He has operated a general equine practice in northern Connecticut since 1979. The primarily ambulatory practice has a clinic that handles emergency care, internal medicine cases, and minor surgery. Dr. Werner's special interests include lameness, prepurchase examinations, wellness care, and owner education. Dr. Werner is the 2008 president-elect of the American Association of Equine Practitioners (AAEP). He has held positions as AAEP treasurer, chair of the AAEP Purchase Examination Committee, and president of the Connecticut Veterinary Medical Association. He has made presentations at AAEP conventions on lameness in sport horses and prepurchase examinations and served on numerous panels including lameness in sport horses and Lyme disease. He has coauthored publications on equine Lyme disease and prepurchase examination guidelines and writes frequently for industry publications.

Must-Know Info
Signs of Colic

The word "colic" strikes fear in horse owners' hearts. What exactly is this dreaded condition and how can you recognize its early signs before your horse's life is at risk? Read on.

❧

"Colic" is used to describe the nonspecific pain in the belly suffered by infants as well as horses—creatures who can't tell us where it hurts. In ninety percent of cases, it is the result of something stopping the flow of food through the intestinal tract. Causes include impacted feces, gas, a foreign object, an enterolith (a stone that has formed in the intestine), parasites (usually a problem in weanling horses), or strangulated bowel. The remaining ten percent of colic cases are caused by infectious disease.

Recognizing the early signs of colic is crucial in treating it. Know your horse's normal behavior so you can tell when he's not acting as he should. Colic pain can go from mild to severe in a very short time, and you want to be able to catch any changes in behavior quickly.

A horse's entire belly will be painful even if only one part of his intestines is affected. This is why a lack of interest in food or water is often an early sign of colic. As the pain worsens, the horse may sweat, dig with his front hooves, or look around at his flanks. He will

get up and down frequently and turn around in his stall as the
pain becomes more severe. If he isn't treated, his behavior will
become more violent as the pain becomes unbearable.

Rolling is one of the most well known signs of colic, and
it looks different from when a horse rolls to scratch his back
in a hard-to-reach place. Horses with colic roll erratically
and repeatedly and oftentimes all the way over from side to
side.

If you see your horse begin to show early signs of colic, call
your veterinarian right away. Note the time his symptoms began
as well as how much manure is in his stall. Your veterinarian will
need this information as he works to help your horse.

Dealing with a colicking horse is a terrifying experience for most
owners. Anyone who has gone through the experience will agree
that prevention is a much better option. Horse owners can do a lot
to prevent the common causes of colic. The most important and
effective management strategy is to keep the horse in as natural
an environment as possible. This means frequent or permanent
turnout, a predominantly forage diet, and regular exercise.

Horses evolved on the American plains, where they ate forage
for many hours a day. Reproducing this environment as closely
as possible helps to keep a modern-day horse's digestive system
working properly.

Of course, not every owner has the option of providing pasture, but there are other measures you can take. Provide your
horse with as much living space as possible and encourage him
to move. Try to fulfill his dietary needs with grass hay alone. Add
grain only if necessary to maintain his body condition.

Frequency of feeding is also important. A horse's digestive tract is meant to take in food continuously. So the more frequently you can feed your horse, the better. Give smalls amounts more often, or feed with a safe hay net to encourage him to eat more slowly.

Make certain your horse has adequate water to drink. Even if there is a nice pond in his pasture, he may not always use it. Encourage him to drink by adding a water trough. Temperature extremes can also discourage drinking. If the weather is hot, make sure your horse's water is cool. In wintertime, if the water is very cold, warm it with a heater.

The link between exercise and gut movement is not well understood, but there seems to be a connection. Horses who live in the wild, where colic seems to be uncommon, continually move as they eat. It may be that the equine brain connects body movement with gut movement. Even if your horse can't move around while he's eating in his stall, getting him out every day and providing him with exercise will help keep his digestive tract functioning normally.

Maintaining your horse at an optimal weight can also reduce the likelihood of colic. Overweight horses have greater difficulty exercising. They are also predisposed to endocrine abnormalities, which can interfere with normal gut function.

Anthony T. Blikslager, D.V.M., Ph.D., Diplomate American College of Veterinary Surgeons, is professor of equine surgery at the North Carolina State University College of Veterinary Medicine. An internationally recognized expert in the field of equine gastrointestinal health, he has published more than 100 veterinary and scientific articles as well as numerous book chapters on colic. His focus is on studying the mechanisms of adverse effects of nonsteroidal anti-inflammatory drugs on the intestine.

Must-Know Info
Keeping Your Horse Happy During a Layup Experience

One of the more challenging aspects of horse ownership is keeping your equine buddy reasonably happy when he's laid up—confined to stall rest so he can heal from an injury. Layups over an extended period are particularly challenging because a horse whose needs aren't adequately met is at a high risk of having healing prolonged, developing stomach ulcers and colic from stress, and reinjuring himself.

Horses are big, active, highly social creatures. Keeping one contentedly confined to a small area takes some effort and creative thinking. Here are some suggestions to consider:

Before the layup begins, be certain you fully understand your veterinarian's instructions so you can be prepared. Find out the dimensions of your horse's stall. We all have various ideas about what's necessary for stall rest, but there is a big difference between a twelve-foot by twelve-foot stall and a twelve-foot by twenty-four-foot stall.

Provide your horse with the biggest area your veterinarian will allow. Horses need and like as much room as possible. If your vet gives the okay, a stall with a run is best. If, however, your horse must be confined to a smaller area, access to a similarly sized outdoor pen will allow you to take him out once in a while so he can enjoy the outdoors. Portable panels are great for this. They make it possible to create a nice twelve-foot by twelve-foot stall anywhere.

Take a close look at the stall where your horse will be living. Check that the flooring is safe and easy to clean. Make sure the flooring is level and can be kept that way. A horse who stands for long periods on a floor with a pit in the center can quickly get sore. If the floor seems uneven, add stall mats. Remember, too, that a horse kept in a stall with a dirt floor can be forced to breathe ammonia from urine when his living quarters aren't properly maintained. This can wreck havoc with his respiratory system.

Light during layup is important, too. Like people, horses can get depressed when kept in a dark, boring environment for a long time. Put your horse in a stall with a window, and keep it open whenever possible to give him fresh air as well as a view. If you have to add lights inside the barn, keep them on a timer so your horse has regular daylight and night photoperiods. This is crucial for proper rest.

An automatic waterer can be a problem during layup because a horse who is trying to amuse himself may use it as a toy and flood his stall. A water bucket may be best for delivering the liquid ration of a convalescing animal who is very curious and easily bored.

Horses are social creatures, and satisfying the needs of your equine buddy's gregarious nature may be your biggest challenge while he's laid up. When possible, put a horse in the stall next to him or across the aisle. Give him a ball or other toys to occupy him. See him as often as possible; numerous short visits are more helpful than infrequent long ones. Playing soothing music for your horse really does seem to make a difference, too.

A horse who is unable to exercise requires fewer calories. If he's kept on the same diet that he received while in training, he'll end up chubby and hyper. Talk to your veterinarian about decreasing the calories, energy content, and amount of your horse's feed while he's laid up. Small, frequent meals are far better than two large feedings a day: they benefit the gastrointestinal tract of an animal designed to graze and help to prevent boredom.

Serving hay in a safe, high-quality hay net can make eating more challenging and prolong mealtime so that your horse gets a little mental exercise in addition to his food. Good quality grass hays are best or add beet pulp to provide extra fiber. Don't give your horse concentrates or pellets unless your veterinarian recommends them or your horse has special dietary needs. Try to keep alfalfa to a minimum if you feed any at all. You'll reduce your horse's energy level and have less urine to clean up.

Take the time to groom your laid-up horse whenever you can. He may prefer not rolling in a small area and will appreciate being brushed and scratched since he can't do it himself. If possible, also remove his shoes, but remember to keep his feet trimmed. Poorly balanced or untrimmed hooves can be very uncomfortable for a confined horse.

Layup is also a wonderful time to teach your horse stretching exercises. Ask your veterinarian which ones are beneficial for your horse, and use a carrot to encourage him to stretch. Also ask your vet about massage or acupressure therapy that will aid healing or simply make your horse feel better. Confined horses really appreciate massage. It can ease the soreness that may result from standing in a small area for an extended time. It also provides mental stimulation.

I don't recommend sedatives or tranquilizers during layup unless absolutely imperative for healing and to prevent further injury. I have found Traditional Chinese Veterinary Medicine prescriptions to be very safe and effective in helping to keep horses calm during this stressful time. Combined with acupuncture, they support the healing process.

When it's time to start your horse on a hand-walking program or turn him out in the pasture, be certain you fully understand your veterinarian's instructions. A confined horse can go bonkers when finally allowed turnout, so be careful. Gradually increase hand-walking times to help expel some of that pent-up energy before turning him loose.

If you can't provide your horse with adequate care and housing while he's convalescing, find a good layup or rehabilitation facility that can fulfill his needs. Keep in mind that layup is not a passive undertaking. Your horse is actively trying to heal from illness or injury, and layup is an integral part of getting him back in action. Using layup in a positive way not only will facilitate healing, but will enhance the relationship you and your horse share, adding a new creative facet that will have lasting benefits.

Kate Gentry-Running, D.V.M., C.V.A., is a practicing veterinarian with twenty-seven years of experience and an emphasis in equine integrative medicine. She received her veterinary degree in 1980 from the University of Missouri College of Veterinary Medicine. In 2001 she was certified by the International Veterinary Acupuncture Society and is currently pursuing a master's degree in Traditional Chinese Veterinary Medicine at the Chi Institute in Gainesville, Florida. Dr. Running breeds and trains cutting horses at her ranch in Tolar, Texas. She is the coauthor of *Horse Health & Nutrition for Dummies*.

Must-Know Info
Shoot Your Horse:
With a Camera, Of Course!

The advent of digital photography has inspired a new generation of hob-byists and encouraged the film generation to go digital. But whatever the differences in the two formats—primarily convenience and saving money on film-developing costs—the same rules of photography still apply. Whether you are taking pictures to share with friends, to regis-ter your horse with a breed organization, or just for fun, try these tips to get the most flattering and appealing images.

Safety first! Practice before you shoot, and be sure your horse is comfortable with his environment. Acclimate him to the sound of your camera. Even the calmest horse can be unpredictable; explain to all children and handlers beforehand how to react if your horse spooks or startles.

Pay attention to details. If you did not thread the end strap of your horse's halter into the keeper, you might not notice it during the shoot, but you will definitely see it when the photo is framed and hanging on your wall. Properly position and safely secure all tack prior to photographing a horse wearing a saddle and bridle.

Have you horse looking his best. He should be in good condition and well groomed. Check him from top to bottom for anything that detracts from his appearance, including a tangled tail, grass stains, and dirt in the corner of his eye.

Coordinate clothing and tack. Check that the rider's attire as well as all tack—the bridle, saddle and pad, and anything else the horse is wearing—complement him. Avoid harsh colors that clash with his coat.

Watch your backgrounds. Think neutral. Look for a canopy of trees or an open field, not a cluttered tack area. Remove all traffic cones, garden hoses, and buckets and repair broken fence boards. Carefully position your horse so that no trees or telephone poles in the background appear to be growing from his head or back. You might be able to remove such distractions with photo-editing software, but it's easier to steer clear of them in the first place.

Avoid harsh glare and unflattering shadows. Shoot during the first and last few hours of the day. The golden hue of morning and evening sunlight is flattering to both horses' coats and people's skin tones.

Capture your horse's attention. For portraits and conformation photos he should be alert with his ears pricked forward. Horses will respond with interest to rustling bags, mirrors, and squeaking toys, but beware: each trick will "get ears" only a few times before a horse is desensitized to it. If your equine subject pays no attention to props, have a helper lead another horse nearby or simply wait for something to pique his interest. It may be as simple as a person getting out of a car.

Be patient. If your horse does something cute and you miss it, don't despair. Chances are, if you're patient and keep your camera ready, you'll catch an encore. Let your model be your muse. If your horse is not in the mood for portraits, take photos of him playing in his pasture. Feeding time is not an optimal opportunity for portraits, but you can get lovely shots of him grazing with the herd.

Minimize motion blur. In action shots use the "sport/action" setting on your camera or shutter priority. Generally, your shutter speed needs to be between 1/250 and 1/1000 of a second to freeze a moving horse's action. As his speed increases, so should your shutter speed.

Maintain his proportions. Lens distortion occurs when you shoot your horse at close range with a wide lens angle. His head appears huge, his body long, and his legs short. Avoid lens distortion and keep your horse in proportion by moving back a few steps and zooming in. Put your camera into the telephoto (zoom) range and shoot at a focal length of 100 millimeters or more.

Get into position. For conformation photos, shoot with the sun at your back and your horse in profile in front of you. Keep your camera at the level of his shoulder.

Experiment with your camera. Rules are made to be broken. See what sorts of images you get if you shoot toward the sun or from a wacky angle. Practice lighting effects with inanimate objects, such as stuffed animals and model horses, so you can work on the perfect silhouette without worrying about how long your model will cooperate. The beauty of digital photography is that you can delete any "oops" images.

Your camera is just the first step to a great photograph. Basic picture-editing software can do more than fix errors. You can also adjust colors, contrast, sharpness, and more, or use special brush tools effects to create digital paintings.

When you've decided to share your new skills with the world and submit photos to contests and publications, first check the submission guidelines for rules regarding photo size as well as manipulation.

So get out there with that camera, whether it's a pint-sized point-and-shoot or a more sophisticated digital SLR model. The biggest differences between professional and amateur images are background, details, lighting, and the positioning of your subject. Once you have mastered capturing an effective image, you'll be amazed at the difference. The result: great pictures of your horse that you'll want to keep, print, and share.

Sarah K. Andrew is a New Jersey-based photographer specializing in equine subjects. Her work has been featured in many publications, including the *New York Times*, and proudly hangs framed on many a horse owner's wall. Her website is www.rockandracehorses.com.

Must-Know Info
Saddle Fit Secrets Unraveled

Using a saddle that properly fits your horse is of crucial importance. A poor-fitting saddle can cause pain that results in performance and behavior problems.

To determine if a saddle fits your horse, have him stand squarely on level ground. Put the saddle on without a pad and without tightening the girth or cinch. From the ground, check the following ten elements of saddle fit:

1. Saddle Placement

Find the sweet spot—the place on your horse where the saddle nestles in and feels most secure. Do not place it too far forward onto his neck or too far back onto his croup. The position should be one to three inches behind the back of the shoulder blade for an English saddle and slightly overlapping the shoulder on a Western saddle. Although a Western saddletree is longer and often overlaps the back of the shoulder blade by several inches, a properly fitting one should still allow free movement of the shoulder.

If you are not sure of proper saddle position, place it really far forward and then push it lightly back toward the horse's rear end. You will feel a place where the saddle wants to stop. This is the correct position for that horse. Repeat the process to make sure the saddle stops in the same place each time.

Many riders place their saddles too far forward, restricting the movement of the horse's shoulder. The equine shoulder blade moves backward as much as three inches when a horse is in motion, so saddle placement must allow enough clearance for the shoulder to move freely without running into the tree.

2. Correct Tree Angles

The front angle of the saddletree is one of the most important aspects of evaluating a saddle's suitability for a particular horse. When the angle of the tree does not match the angle (slope) of the horse's shoulders, the saddle does not fit.

On an English saddle, lift up the saddle flaps and look for the points of the tree. On most saddles you can see what looks like a leather pocket. Inside this pocket, under the leather, lie the points of the saddle. This is the end of the front of the tree. The Western tree is easier to locate since it is hidden only by sheepskin underneath and leather on top.

With the saddle in place on the horse, look at and feel the angle of the front of the tree from where it starts to touch him on either side of the spine down to the lower end of the point or bar. Compare it to the angle of the horse's body. If the tree angle is parallel to his body, the tree is the correct angle for the horse. If the angle of the points is narrower than the angle of the horse's body, the tree is too narrow. If the angle is wider, it's too wide.

When the angle is too narrow, the saddle will pinch the horse at the bottom of the points, causing discomfort. If the tree is too wide, it either will fall down on top of the withers, creating little or no gullet clearance or, once loaded, it will fall down in front, putting pressure at the top of the tree angle.

3. Consistent Contact

Apply some pressure to simulate having a rider in the saddle. Place a flat hand into the front of the tree and run it from the top of the tree angle to the bottom, looking for equally consistent pressure. Check both sides of your horse because he may be different on each side.

Next, insert your hand into the gullet opening—the part that sits above the tree or panels—and then to the side of the spine to check for consistent contact with the tree (or panels) from front to back under the length of the tree. If you feel less contact (extra space) in the middle, the saddle is bridging, which means it is not touching the horse in the middle.

An English tree has more give to it so a little bridging may go away when a rider is aboard. But a Western saddletree should have no give. If a Western saddle bridges without a rider, it will bridge with one. This will cause a horse pain as the tree displaces all the rider's weight only to the front and back of the tree.

Also check for rocking, which concentrates the rider's weight in the middle of the horse's back, reducing the area of support and often causing soreness. With a hand on the pommel (the front) and the other on the cantle (the back), alternately press down with one hand and then the other. If the saddle rocks excessively on the center of the tree, the saddle may not fit; in an English saddle, the flocking probably needs to be adjusted.

4. Saddle Balance

On most English saddles, the cantle is designed to sit one to two inches higher than the pommel. Most Western saddles are designed so that the pommel and cantle are roughly even.

If the front is higher in either type of saddle, the tree may be too narrow. Likewise, if the front is too low, the tree may be too wide. Whether a saddle sits a little high or low in front or back, one that properly fits always has a level flat spot in the seat so the rider is not fighting the seat to stay balanced on the horse.

5. Level Seat

With the saddle correctly placed on the horse's back, look for the lowest point of the seat. In most cases, this is a level area centered between the pommel and cantle. This is the ideal position because it allows a rider to sit comfortably balanced and effectively deliver seat and leg aids without shifting his weight to the front or back of the tree.

When the flat spot is too far back or, worse, there is no flat spot and the seat looks like a wide V, the rider tips back toward the cantle, shifting all his weight to the back of the panels or bars. This causes the horse to hollow his back. If the saddle's center is too far forward, the rider slides toward the pommel and feels out of balance.

If either of these balance flaws exit, the rider's natural response is to brace with his legs, making the aids less effective and causing an unstable feel for both rider and horse.

A seat that is not level may indicate a serious saddle-fit problem or maybe the saddle was not designed to have a balanced seat.

As long as the saddletree correctly fits the horse, it may be possible to adjust the balance with wool flocking in an English saddle or with shims or padding in a Western model. However, if the saddle is built to sit you in some other position (which is common for specialty riding situations like racing or reining), it will be easier to start over with a better saddle for your needs.

6. Wither and Spine Clearance

With no rider in the saddle, you should be able to fit three fingers into the gullet space between the bottom of the pommel and the horse's withers without feeling cramped.

If there isn't sufficient room, but the tree angle fits, a saddle fitter may be able to add flocking to an English saddle or shims to a Western saddle to ensure that it clears the horse's withers.

With a rider in the saddle, there needs to be at least two fingers (two inches) of space to assure that the tree is not able to put pressure directly on the horse's spine.

Look down the gullet—from the front and from the rear, if you can. It should clear the entire length of the horse's spine by two to three inches.

7. Stability

With no pad, cinch up the saddle and check for excessive movement side to side. Look at the saddle from all angles to make sure the gullet lines up with the horse's topline. Horses may be asymmetrical and so might a saddle. Closely check to make sure any unevenness is not causing an issue with this horse-saddle combination.

8. Correct Bar Length

The weight-bearing surface of a saddle should be from two inches behind the horse's shoulder blades to the point where his last rib meets his spine. To find this point, locate his last rib and follow it to the spine. If the saddle sits behind this point, it will rest on the lumbar region—the weakest part of a horse's back—where it can cause injury.

9. Horse's Response

Every horse is inherently honest. No horse ever lies about saddle fit, so listen to him. His movements and actions will tell you whether he is comfortable. This is the acid test of saddle fitting.

A horse who moves freely, calmly, without hesitation or rushing is probably wearing a saddle that fits him correctly. Most horses show an immediate, dramatic change in disposition and movement when an ill-fitting saddle is fixed or replaced with one that fits well.

When a horse just isn't going right, his back, feet, and teeth are the most important places to look for clues to answer why. Your veterinarian, your farrier, and your saddle fitter will be your best allies in helping you determine what is creating problems in your horse.

10. Repeat Elements 1–9 While Riding

This is the final test once you have a saddle that you think fits. Saddle up with a thin pad and check how all of the above-mentioned elements fare with a rider's weight and while the horse is moving.

Susan and David Hartje own and operate Saddles That Fit!, an educationally focused, independent saddle-fitting business in northern California. Since 2002, they have traveled throughout the West helping horse owners understand how to check saddle fit and assisting them in finding Western, English, and endurance saddles that fit both them and their horses. More detailed saddle-fitting information can be found on their website www.saddlesthatfit.com.

Our equine friends always give us a reason to smile.

A lowered head usually
indicates a relaxed horse.

A horse's chest is very muscular, allowing for quick bursts of energy for running.

What do you give a horse for his birthday? Carrot cake, of course.

This appaloosa looks ready for gymkana, a western sporting competition.

Accessorizing is important for this fashion forward horse.

Horses usually have a
life expectancy of
twenty-five to
thirty years, but
they live in our
hearts forever.

Western discipline horses learn to neck reign, where the rider holds the reign in one hand, and pushes on the opposite side to indicate where to go.

Must-Know Info
Combating Flies

There's a saying: "God made the fly but forgot to tell us why."

We've sort of figured it out, though, and although any fly-hating horse or horse owner may find it hard to fathom, most flies aren't so bad. The majority play an important role as scavengers while other flies are responsible for pollinating many wild and cultivated plants. The number of fly species that bother horses is actually small.

So which flies make life miserable around the stable and what can you do about them? Here's the lineup of flying pests found around horses:

Stable flies. The biggest flying culprit is the stable fly. In the last 30 years, it has become the number one pest fly of horses and cattle in pastures. Stable flies develop in decomposing plant matter, aging horse feces, spilled feed, grass clippings, and silage. They inflict painful bites to the legs and belly that are thirty to forty times worse than the bite of a mosquito. It's no surprise then that horses swish and stomp them away—only to send them to annoy another nearby animal.

Sanitation is the best means of controlling stable flies. Work to reduce or eliminate places for fly larvae in and around the stable and apply insecticides to surfaces where flies rest. (Look for black fecal spots the flies leave behind to find these resting areas.) Poisoned fly baits, although effective against house flies, are not effective against stable flies because their piercing-sucking mouthparts don't allow them to feed on the bait.

Parasitic wasps can also be helpful in keeping stable-fly populations down. These wasps feed on the fly pupae, killing the fly before it has a chance to mature.

When sprayed on a horse's legs and belly, pesticide containing permethrin (a pyrethroid) can help reduce the annoyance of stable flies. The spray is especially effective if the horse doesn't come in contact with grasses and other plants that can brush it off.

Face flies. These pests feed on a horse's eye secretions and irritate the eyes with their long, sharp teeth and sponging mouthparts. Face flies develop in fresh cow manure, but not in horse dung, which means your horse has cattle to thank for these miserable pests.

The most effective way to control face flies is to cover your horse's face with a fly mask. Available in a variety of styles, most use netting to shield the eyes from flies. Insecticidal wipes aren't an effective deterrent unless used very close to the eyes—in which case, they're not safe for horses.

Houseflies. The common housefly is as happy to hang around livestock as your home's trash container. They develop in livestock feces as well as in decomposing plant material such as rotting silage or grass clippings. These flies have sponging mouthparts but no sharp teeth, so they don't inflict physical damage while feeding on their hosts. However, they can spread disease to both animals and people. They can carry bacteria and other pathogenic organisms on their mouthparts and in their feces and can contaminate human and animal food. To control housefly populations, keep your horse's stall and pasture clean. One pound of manure can produce 454 flies, so removing it promptly is essential to controlling these pests.

Horn flies. They may look like half-sized houseflies, but horn flies have their own distinctive behavior. They use a small piercing-sucking proboscis to feed on the blood of their hosts, which most often are cattle. They will bother horses that are stabled near cattle, however. These pests can pierce their hosts' skin up to thirty-five times a day, causing irritation and blood loss. They develop in fresh cow manure, but not in horse manure. They can often be found accumulating on horses' backs, where their bites can be seen.

Insecticidal wipes and sprays made for use on horses can be used to fight horn flies. By practicing good manure management and using fly cover-ups, parasitic wasps, and fly wipes and sprays, horse owners can do a lot to protect their equine companions from flies.

Alberto B. Broce, Ph.D., is a professor of entomology at Kansas State University. He has committed his career to researching insects that affect man and animals. They range from flies and fleas to ticks and mites. Dr. Broce is an expert on flies of veterinary importance, especially stable flies, houseflies, face flies, and horn flies. He has done research on insecticide resistance, trapping methods, migration patterns, breeding habits, and control strategies for flies and other pests.

Common Horse Terms

Ever been in a room full of horsepeople and had trouble keeping up with the conversation? Knowing these commonly used horse terms can help you sound like a pro the next time around.

bit—device, usually made of metal, that is placed in a horse's mouth; attached to the bridle and reins.

bombproof—horse that is not easily spooked.

canter— a term used in English riding to describe a three-beat gait with right or left leads.

cribber—horse that compulsively clenches the edge of an object with his teeth and gulps air through his mouth.

English—style of tack and attire as well as particular riding styles, most of which require riders to use both hands on the reins.

farrier—a skilled professional who trims and/or shoes the feet of horses.

fetlock—lower leg joint that projects above and behind the hoof.

forelock—mane hair that comes between the ears and rests on the forehead.

founder—internal deformity of a horse's hoof caused by detachment and rotation of one of the bones within it; produces severe lameness.

gelding—male horse that has had his testicles removed.

girth—strap used to hold a saddle or harness in place; positioned around a horse's body just behind his front legs.

gymkhana—timed rodeo events, including barrel racing and pole bending.

hackamore—bridle that utilizes a nosepiece in place of a bit.

halter—harness that fits over a horse's head.

hock—joint at approximately the midpoint of a horse's back leg; corresponds to the human ankle.

lead—the foreleg that extends beyond and strikes the ground ahead of the other foreleg at the lope or canter.

lead rope—rope with a snap on one end; attached to a halter to lead or tie a horse.

lope—the Western term for a slow canter.

mare—female horse older than four.

pastern—area between the fetlock joint and hoof.

poll—area between the ears; the highest point of a horse's head.

pony—a small breed of horse usually less than 14.2 hands (58 inches) in height.

post—to rise from the saddle and return to it in rhythm with a horse's trot.

proud flesh—excessive growth of granulation tissue that delays or halts wound healing.

purebred—horse whose sire and dam are of the same breed.

reins—straps attached to the bit and held by a rider to control a horse.

stallion—uncastrated male horse older than four.

stud—stallion used for breeding.

tack—variety of equipment used on a horse; includes brushes, blankets, bridles, halters, saddles, and other items.

thoroughbred—distinct equine breed developed for racing; the term is not interchangeable with "purebred."

trot—two-beat diagonal gait.

weanling—young horse (foal) that has just been weaned from its mother.

Western—style of tack and attire commonly associated with the American West; riders most often hold the reins in one hand.

yearling—horse or pony that is one year old.

Resources

American Horse Defense Fund, Inc. (AHDF), 1718 M Street, NW, Unit 191, Washington, DC 20036-4504, 866-956-AHDF (2433), www.ahdf.org

The AHDF was formed in 2000 for the purpose of helping to end the mistreatment of horses and other equines. Based in Washington, DC, the group provides lobbying efforts to support anticruelty legislation and works to educate the public about equine welfare. Recent efforts include working toward passage of antislaughter legislation, stronger penalties against the soring of gaited show horses, and the humane treatment of wild horses.

American Miniature Horse Association (AMHA), 5601 South Interstate 35 W, Alvarado, TX 76009, 817-783-5600, www.amha.org

The governing body for the miniature horse in America, the AMHA sanctions shows and provides a central promotional source for the breed. Miniature horses are shown in driving classes as well as in halter and liberty classes. The organization's bimonthly magazine highlights the breed's successes.

American Morgan Horse Association (AMHA), 122 Bostwick Road, Shelburne, VT 05482-4417, 802-985-4944, www.morganhorse.com

Morgan horses are registered by the AMHA, an organization devoted to preserving and promoting this uniquely American breed. The group publishes a monthly magazine and sponsors a versatility program that promotes using the breed in a variety of disciplines.

American Paint Horse Association (APHA), P.O. Box 961023, Fort Worth, TX 76161-0023, 817-834-APHA (2742), www.apha.com

The APHA is the registering body for the American paint horse, one of the most popular breeds in the United States. The organization sponsors shows and paint horse racing and promotes the breed around the world. *The Paint Horse Journal* is the organization's award-winning monthly magazine.

American Quarter Horse Association (AQHA), P.O. Box 200, Amarillo, TX 79168, 800-414-RIDE (7433), www.aqha.com

If the stories, photos, and information in this book have inspired you to take the next step and become more involved with horses, AQHA can help through its professional horsemen and breeder referral services. AQHA has several programs and offers real options for the horse-loving public, especially the casual horse lover who is thinking of taking the next step. Whether you are planning a vacation and would like to include horses or you need information on how to purchase a horse, find a trainer or a veterinarian, the AQHA is ready to help you discover how special horses can be. To acquaint you with horse ownership, AQHA offers a free DVD (a $5 shipping charge applies) entitled *Owning Your First American Quarter Horse.* Call or write AQHA to get your copy.

Appaloosa Horse Club (ApHC), 2720 West Pullman Road, Moscow, ID 83843, 208-882-5578, www.appaloosa.com

Located in Idaho, where the appaloosa is considered the official state horse, the ApHC registers these spotted horses and produces a monthly publication. The organization also sanctions breed-specific shows and holds annual trail rides.

Arabian Horse Association (AHA), 10805 E. Bethany Drive, Aurora, CO 80014, 303-696-4500, www.arabianhorses.org

The Arabian horse is one of the oldest breeds in the world. The AHA registers these horses in the United States and sponsors a variety of programs for this versatile breed. The organization sponsors a monthly magazine and has set up a foundation to help support various aspects of the equine industry.

Tennessee Walking Horse Breeders' and Exhibitors' Association (TWHBEA), P.O. Box 286, Lewisburg, TN 37091, 931-359-1574, www.twhbea.com

The TWHBEA is the oldest registering body for the Tennessee walking horse. The organization holds breed-specific shows and promotes use of the Tennessee walking horse in many different disciplines, including dressage, endurance, and driving. The group also encourages members to host trail rides around the country for Tennessee walking horses.

American Society for the Prevention of Cruelty to Animals (ASPCA), 424 E. 92nd Street, New York, NY 10128-6804, 212-876-7700, www.aspca.org

Founded in 1866, the ASPCA aims to prevent cruelty and alleviate the pain, fear, and suffering of animals by providing local and national programs that assist thousands of animals nationwide. The ASPCA's national programs include the animal poison control center, humane education, companion animal services, and the national shelter outreach program.

American Veterinary Medical Association (AVMA), 1931 N. Meacham Road, Suite 100, Schaumburg, IL 60173-4360, 847-925-8070, www.avma.org

The AVMA, founded in 1863, is one of the oldest and largest veterinary medical organizations in the world. Its more than 76,000 member veterinarians recognize the importance of the human–animal bond and the veterinarian's role in preserving, protecting, and strengthening relationships between people and animals. AVMA members contribute to the health and well-being of people and animals through work in clinical practice, public health, regulatory agencies, uniformed services, and research.

Delta Society, 875 124th Ave. NE, Suite 101, Bellevue, WA 98005-2531, 425-679-5500, www.deltasociety.org

The Delta Society's mission is to improve human health through service and therapy animals. The organization works to expand awareness of the positive effects animals can have on human health, reduce barriers that prevent the involvement of animals in everyday life, and expand the therapeutic and service role of animals in human health, service, and education. Delta Pet Partners volunteers visit hospitals, nursing homes, schools, hospices, and other facilities with their pets, providing animal-assisted activities and therapy throughout the United States and the world. The Pet Partners program registers all types of pets, including dogs, cats, rabbits, birds, horses, and other domestic animals.

Equine Rescue League (ERL), P.O. Box 4366, Leesburg, VA 20177, 540-822-4577, www.equinerescueleague.org

The ERL is a nonprofit organization that supports the responsible use of working, sport and pleasure horses, ponies, donkeys, and mules. Its goals are to prevent the neglect or abuse of any equine, to offer educational programs to the community, and to provide shelter, rehabilitation, and adoption for those animals in need of its services.

Humane Society of the United States (HSUS), 2100 L Street, NW, Washington, DC 20037, 202-452-1100, www.hsus.org

The HSUS, the nation's largest animal-protection organization, supports shelters and pet owners in building and enhancing the human-companion-animal bond through its Pets for Life campaign. Pets for Life provides solutions—to behavior issues, restrictions on rental housing, and the concerns of allergic, pregnant, or immunocompromised individuals. It also promotes humane animal care and adoption to end the relinquishment, abandonment, and euthanasia of healthy dogs and cats.

Morris Animal Foundation (MAF), 10200 East Girard Ave., B430, Denver, CO 80231, 800-243-2345, www.morrisanimalfoundation.org

Established in 1948, the MAF is dedicated to funding research that protects, treats, and cures companion animals and wildlife. MAF has been at the forefront of funding breakthrough research studies benefiting animals in some 100 countries, spanning all seven continents on Earth. Headquartered in Denver, Colorado, the MAF has funded nearly 1,400 humane animal health studies with funds totaling more than $51 million.

North American Riding for the Handicapped Association, Inc. (NARHA), P.O. Box 33150, Denver, CO 80233, 800-369-RIDE (7433), www.narha.org

Since 1969, NARHA has provided Equine Assisted Activity and Therapy (EAAT) programs in the United States and Canada. Through its network of nearly 800 member centers, more than 38,000 individuals with disabilities benefit from activities that include therapeutic riding, hippotherapy, equine assisted psychotherapy, driving, interactive vaulting, and competition. The association ensures its standards are met through an accreditation process for centers and a certification process for instructors. A section of NARHA, the Equine Facilitated Mental Health Association, founded in 1996, provides equine-facilitated psychotherapy (EFP) for people with psychological issues and mental health needs, including anxiety, depression, and autism. EFP is facilitated by a licensed, credentialed mental-health professional who works with an appropriately credentialed equine professional or is dually credentialed as an equine professional.

PetConnection.com, www.PetConnection.com

The online home of Marty Becker, D.V.M., "America's veterinarian," and his writing partner, Gina Spadafori. The two are syndicated columnists and top-selling pet-care authors. Together with other members of the PetConnection team, they offer pet lovers a free searchable library of top-quality pet medical and behavior advice as well as other resources, including newsletters and contests. Every day the PetConnection.com blog provides pet lovers with must-read news on the latest in pet health and animal advocacy. PetConnection.com's affiliated sites, including DogCars.com, also offer free reviews of new vehicles and travel advice for dog lovers.

Race Track Chaplaincy of America (RTCA), P.O. Box 91640, Los Angeles, CA 90009, 310-419-1640, www.racetrackchaplaincy.org

A 501(c)(3) nonprofit corporation chartered in 1971, RTCA sanctions and oversees chaplains who serve at racetracks and training and breeding centers throughout North America and around the world. RTCA provides for the spiritual, emotional, physical, social, and educational needs of horse racing's vast workforce. It provides food, blankets, bedding, and emergency funds to track workers. It also offers a wealth of social services to backstretch workers, including hosting Alcoholics Anonymous (AA) meetings and English as a Second Language (ESL) and computer-learning classes. The RTCA advocates for workers and acts as a liaison between community and racing-related organizations and authorities, including track stewards, track executives and horsemen's associations. RTCA is the only national organization whose sole purpose is to enrich the lives of racing's workforce, particularly those 150,000 persons who live on our nation's backstretches.

University of Florida (UF), Amanda M. House, DVM, Diplomate ACVIM, Assistant Professor, Large Animal Clinical Sciences, PO Box 100136, Gainesville, FL 32610, 352-392-2212, http://vetmed.ufl.edu/extension/equine

Dr. Amanda House, our consultant for *The Ultimate Horse Lover*, serves as the liaison between UF's College of Veterinary Medicine and the horse industry, horse owners, veterinarians, and county faculty in Florida. She develops educational programs and consults on equine health and disease, teaches veterinary and pre-veterinary students, promotes and disseminates information on equine research, and works on the large animal medicine service in the hospital.

Dr. House also serves on the board of directors of the Florida Association of Equine Practitioners and on the horse owner education committee of the American Association of Equine Practitioners. She owns a Thoroughbred mare and enjoys competing in the hunter divisions.

Dr. House coordinates the UF Veterinary Medical Center's annual Healthy Horses Conference on Successful Equine Health Care. The educational day focuses on equine health care for horse owners and enthusiasts and includes lectures, tours of the hospital, and live equine treadmill demonstrations. Registration is always limited, so contact the UF Conference department for more information. The University of Florida is dedicated to providing state of the art medical and surgical care for horses, teaching the future veterinarians of our state, and doing research with the goals of advancing equine wellness in our state and throughout the world.

The Writers

Lynn Allen writes a weekly column about rural life for small town newspapers. *Horse Sense* is one of those columns and has been selected to be part of Lynn's next book, *More Life Out Here.* For more of Lynn's work, visit www.cherawpublishing.com.

Sarah K. Andrew is one of the most talented young equine photographers to debut in years. In the last few years, she and her camera have become well-known at New York and New Jersey racetracks and other equine sport venues. Her work has been featured in many publications, including the *New York Times*, and hangs proudly on many a horse owner's wall. The photos in this book are dedicated to the memory of her first horse Alibar. Visit her at www.rockandracehorses.com.

Mark Baus, D.V.M., is president of Fairfield Equine Associates in Newtown, Connecticut. He has spoken at the local and national level on a wide range of equine-related topics including issues of practice management. He has contributed to numerous publications as well, sharing advice on equine health and managing an equine practice. In years past, Dr. Baus enjoyed horse showing and foxhunting. He received his colors with Fairfield County Hounds in 1989.

Anthony T. Blikslager, D.V.M., Ph.D., Diplomate, American College of Veterinary Surgeons, is assistant professor of equine surgery at the North Carolina State University College of Veterinary Medicine. An internationally recognized expert in the field of equine gastrointestinal health, he has published more than 100 veterinary and scientific articles and numerous book chapters on the subject of colic. His focus is on studying the mechanisms of adverse effects of nonsteroidal anti-inflammatory drugs.

Chaplain Ken Boehm joined Race Track Chaplaincy of America (RTCA) in January 1990 as chaplain at Tampa Bay Downs in Tampa, Florida. Previously he had served as associate pastor in Cleveland, Ohio, and as senior pastor in Lutz, Florida. In April 2003, Chaplain Boehm was asked to be the first full-time chaplain at Churchill Downs and its training facility, Trackside, in Louisville, Kentucky. His ministry recently completed the 350-seat Christ Chapel on the Churchill Downs' backstretch. In 2008 RTCA chaplains elected him their representative to the organization's executive committee. He lives in Louisville with his wife, Natalie, and their fourteen-year-old daughter, Bethany.

Alberto B. Broce, Ph.D., is a professor of entomology at Kansas State University. He has committed his career to researching insects that affect man and animals. They range from flies and fleas to ticks and mites. Dr. Broce is an expert on flies of veterinary importance, especially stable flies, houseflies, face flies, and horn flies. He has done research on insecticide resistance, trapping methods, migration patterns, breeding habits, and control strategies for flies and other pests.

Karen Bumgarner is a second-generation horseperson, who grew up with thoroughbred racehorses on the backsides of several northwestern racetracks. Karen's love of trail riding and the backcountry led her to endurance riding in 1977, and she has since ridden almost 20,000 miles on rides sanctioned by the American Endurance Ride Conference (AERC), an accomplishment she shares with fewer than twenty other AERC members since the organization began in 1971. Karen has ridden three horses beyond the 4,000-mile milestone, all with wins and best-condition honors. Karen has written more than 100 articles on endurance riding and horse care and is the author of two books, *America's Long Distance Challenge* and the *Endurance Horse Daily Planner* logbook and journal (both now out of print).

Kathe Campbell lives on a Montana mountain with her mammoth donkeys, a keeshond, and a few kitties. She is a prolific writer on Alzheimer's disease, and her stories are found on many e-zines. Kathe is a contributing author to the Chicken Soup for the Soul series, numerous anthologies, *Rx for Writers*, and medical journals. E-mail Kathe at kathe@wildblue.net.

Chera Cluck is a former jockey and currently full-time trainer of thoroughbreds at Santa Anita. Chera's philosophy that the horse comes first and that they are a gift from God to nurture and protect, isn't what you would expect in the pressure-filled, winner-takes-all-world of horse racing. In addition to her 24/7 work as a trainer, Chera's goal is to establish a foundation dedicated to saving injured racehorses from euthanasia and giving them a second chance at life. You can reach Chera by e-mail at cheracluck@yahoo.com or through the author, at cpepperbytheriver@sbcglobal.net.

Cary Davis is a dressage enthusiast and freelance writer specializing in horse-related articles. Her work has appeared in numerous newspapers and magazines such as *Horse Illustrated*, *Equus*, *Horses USA*, *Quarter Horses USA*, *Hobby Farms*, the *Equine Market*, *Horse and Horseman*, *Midwest Pets*, and *In Stride*. Cary lives near Phoenix, Arizona, with her three quarter horses.

Jennifer DiCamillo has won more than 125 writing awards in the last five years. She writes in every genre and under more than one pseudonym. She bred and trained paint horses for ten years in southern Nevada before breaking her back when a horse flipped over.

Mike Donahue, a retired journalist, and his wife, Linda, own Little Meadows Horse Farm in Overton, Nevada. Donahue has written about the West and its inhabitants for nearly thirty-five years. He is the author of *Mouse's Tank*, an historic novel, and coauthor of the nonfiction *A Day Without Pain*.

Ed Donnally was a jockey for nineteen years, riding at more than fifty tracks and winning more than 1,200 races. He is an Eclipse Award-winning writer, formerly with the *Dallas Morning News*, and has published more than forty articles. An ordained minister and chaplain, he is the associate pastor at Venice Beach Foursquare Church and development director for the Race Track Chaplaincy of America, which sanctions and oversees eighty chaplains who serve at 120 track and training and breeding centers in the United States, Canada, and six other nations. He lives in Los Angeles with his wife, Sandi.

Janet Perez Eckles is a national inspirational speaker and freelance writer. In addition to contributing to ten books, including the Chicken Soup for the Soul series, she authored the inspirational book *Trials of Today, Treasures for Tomorrow: Overcoming Adversities in Life*. You can visit Janet at www.janetperezeckles.com.

Amelia Gagliano is a board-certified music therapist living in northern California with her husband, Gary, two charming house cats, and her Lipizzan stallion Oskar. Amelia and Oskar are partners in classical dressage and students of Dr. Thomas Ritter. For more information on classical dressage and Lipizzans, visit www.whv-lipizzans.com.

Karen Gellman, D.V.M., Ph.D., is a graduate of Cornell College of Veterinary Medicine and has a doctorate from Cornell in animal locomotion biomechanics. She has advanced training and certification in veterinary acupuncture and veterinary chiropractic. She has also studied physical-therapy techniques with some of the leading equine physiotherapists in England and Canada. Dr. Gellman teaches internationally about posture, complementary therapies, and biomechanics; her students are horsemen, veterinarians, and physical therapists. She also is involved with both clinical and basic science research about posture in horses, dogs, and people. Learn about her work and upcoming events at www.equinesportsmed.com, or find a Postural Rehabilitation practitioner at www.posturalrehabvets.com.

Kate Gentry-Running, D.V.M., C.V.A., is a practicing veterinarian with twenty-seven years of experience and an emphasis in equine integrative medicine. She received her veterinary degree in 1980 from the University of Missouri College of Veterinary Medicine. She was certified by the International Veterinary Acupuncture Society in 2001 and is currently pursuing a master's degree in Traditional Chinese Veterinary Medicine at the Chi Institute in Gainesville, Florida. Dr. Running breeds and trains cutting horses at her ranch in Tolar, Texas. She is the coauthor of *Horse Health & Nutrition for Dummies*.

Juliet M. Getty, Ph.D., with Getty Equine Nutrition, is an equine nutritionist in private practice in Haslet, Texas. She earned her master of science degree in animal nutrition at the University of Florida, and completed her doctoral course work in animal nutrition at the University of Georgia. Dr. Getty continued her studies at the University of North Texas, where she earned her Ph.D. Visit the Getty Equine Nutrition website at www.gettyequinenutrition.com

Susan and David Hartje own and operate Saddles That Fit!, an educationally focused, independent saddle-fitting business in northern California. Since 2002, they have traveled throughout the West, helping horse owners understand how to check saddle fit and assisting them in finding Western, English, and endurance saddles that fit both them and their horses. You can find more detailed saddle-fitting information at their website: www.saddlesthatfit.com.

Kim Henneman, D.V.M., C.V.A., C.V.C., is a graduate of Purdue University School of Veterinary Medicine. She is certified by the International Veterinary Acupuncture Society in veterinary acupuncture and veterinary Chinese herbal medicine, and by the American Veterinary Chiropractic Association in veterinary chiropractic—only the twenty-first such certification in the United States. Dr. Henneman's practice is concentrated exclusively in complementary therapies. She has completed training in both basic and advanced classical veterinary homeopathy and has integrated classical homeopathy for both companion and equine patients into her practice since 1994. In 2006 she traveled to China to study Traditional Chinese and Tibetan Veterinary Medicine and is currently working on a master's degree in Traditional Chinese Veterinary Medicine from the Chi Institute and the Southwest University College of Animal Science and Technology in Sichuan, China. Dr. Henneman can be reached by e-mail at AHOoffice@aol.com.

Maureen Joseph is middle-aged, married, with five dogs and six horses and one on the way. She took up reining and breeding her only broodmare for that discipline. Horses are Maureen's life, and the mare in her story still lives with her. She is fat and happy—well, as happy as she can get.

Jacklyn Lee Lindstrom has been a horse lover since day one. For twenty years she and her family raised horses on their small farm in Minnesota. Now retired and living in Spearfish, South Dakota, she finds the stirrups too high and the ground too hard for riding, so she lives her passion for horses through painting and writing.

Kathleen Livingston has enjoyed her intoxicating love for horses for thirty years. She was lucky enough to have Spangled in her life for twelve and a half of his twenty-three years. The love they shared burns in her chest even six years after his passing.

Rolland Love is the author of award-wining short stories, novels, a bestselling computer book, and coauthor of *Homegrown in the Ozarks* with Mary-Lane Kamberg (kansascitywriters.com). Among his acting forays, Rolland played a standardized patient at the University of Kansas School of Medicine, medical healer, monk, villain, Lewis and Clark reenactor, and John Calvin McCoy, founder of Westport, Missouri. Visit Rolland on his website, http://ozarkstories.com.

Don MacDonald Jr. retired from racing and training horses a year after receiving a heart transplant twenty-five years ago. He recently built a home in the country near Eganville, Ontario, where he lives with his wife, Caz. Don is co-owner of the nearby Whitetail Golf Club.

Roberta Thomas Mancuso has had a lifelong love affair with horses and has kept horseback riding a part of her life for more than forty years. She lives in Cheshire, Connecticut, with her supportive husband, Greg, her beautiful (inside and out) daughter, Jessica, two cats, a dog, and, of course, her beloved horse, Sam.

Elizabeth Kaye McCall is passionate about horses, travel, and entertainment. She was the horse-industry liaison for the equestrian spectacle Cavalia on its North American tour. The author of *The Tao Of Horses: Exploring How Horses Guide Us on Our Spiritual Path* (Adams Media, 2004), Elizabeth contributes to many publications including *Dressage Today*, *Cowboys & Indians*, *America's Horse*, *Los Angeles Times*, *Seattle Post-Intelligencer*, and *USA Weekend*. She lives in "Horsetown USA," Norco, California.

Sue McDonnell, M.S., Ph.D., is a board-certified applied animal behaviorist who is a professor and founding head of the Equine Behavior Program at New Bolton Center, University of Pennsylvania School of Veterinary Medicine. Her work includes clinical, research, and teaching activities focused on horse behavior. Her research interests include several areas within equine physiology, behavior, and welfare. In addition to laboratory and field studies, she maintains a semiferal herd of ponies specifically to study their physiology and behavior under seminatural conditions. Dr. McDonnell is the author of two introductory-level books for horse owners on horse behavior, is coeditor of the most current academic book on horse behavior, *The Domestic Horse*, published by Cambridge University Press, and is author of a book and DVD cataloging behavior of horses under both domestic and natural conditions titled, *The Equid Ethogram*. This practical field guide to understanding horse behavior is available at www.horsebehaviordvd.com.

Arthur Montague is a Canadian author of five books and numerous articles and essays in U.S. magazines and anthologies. His latest publication is the *Ottawa Book of Everything* (MacIntyre Purcell Inc.). His website, www.artmontague.com, highlights his writing achievements over the past eight years.

Kelly Mount, her husband, Paul, and their two children reside in Gavilan Hills, California. They own two registered Spanish Mustang geldings; a grullo roan and dun roan, and are partners in a dun roan, registered, Spanish Mustang mare with Wind Walker Ranch. Kelly is a member of the California Colonial Spanish Horse Club (ccshc.org), the Spanish Mustang Registry (spanishmustang.org), and the American Heritage Horse Association (americanheritagehorse.org).

Theresa Peluso is the coauthor of the bestselling *Chicken Soup for the Horse Lover's Soul*, its sequel, *Chicken Soup for the Horse Lover's Soul II*, and several other titles in the Chicken Soup for the Soul series. She is a volunteer at Horses and the Handicapped, a North American Riding for the Handicapped Association (NARHA) premiere accredited facility that provides equine-assisted activities and hippotherapy for physically, emotionally, and cognitively challenged students from ages four to seventy-four on a scholarship basis. For more information, visit www.handhmagic.org and NARHA at www.narha.org.

Carrie Pepper, a freelance writer based in Sacramento, California, has written on a variety of topics, including health and sports, environmental issues, and natural resources, for local and national publications. She is currently working on a collection of short stories (many of which are animal-related) titled *The Nose in the Knothole and Other Stories*, as well as a memoir related to her brother's death in Vietnam. She has rescued and written about cats, dogs, rabbits, and most recently, a California gull. You can read more about Carrie at www.carriepepper.com.

Pauline Peterson is the author of *Horses for Pauline* (Hoofbeat Press, Box 484, Castle Rock, MN, 55010), which is the compilation of her columns from "Horse'n Around," published over a five-year period. Pauline grew up as a city slicker, riding dude-ranch horses. Her life has included many breeds of horses, each expanding her love for horses and enriching the life lessons learned along the way. You can e-mail Pauline at inspire_u@email.com.

Pete Ramey is a natural hoof-care practitioner and author of *Making Natural Hoof Care Work for You* (Star Ridge). He is also the author of numerous articles on the subject of hoof care. He conducts clinics around the country designed to provide a high level of hoof-rehabilitation knowledge and understanding to veterinarians and farriers. For more information, visit www.hoofrehab.com.

Melissa Rice is an award-winning journalist. She is editor of the *Arlington Citizen* (Nebraska) newspaper and assistant editor of the Washington County *Pilot-Tribune* and

Enterprise newspapers. A summa cum laude graduate of the University of Nebraska at Omaha, Melissa is married and enjoys riding and showing American quarter horses.

Monty Roberts, known as "the man who listens to horses" for his *New York Times* best-selling autobiography of the same name, is an award-winning trainer of championship horses and creator of the world-renowned equine training technique called Join-Up. He trains some of Queen Elizabeth II's equestrian team in London and has been awarded an honorary doctorate from the University of Zurich. He continues traveling the globe to spread his message of nonviolence, teaching his techniques to his growing number of students and advising executives at Fortune 500 companies. He can be reached at AskMonty@montyroberts.com.

Jennifer Rowan is the owner of Beardsley Publishing, a family business started in 1962. She took over in 1991, and in 2000 started *Stable Management*, a trade magazine for horse professionals. The idea to publish *Stable Management* grew from her experience running a thirty-stall training and boarding facility with her husband in Connecticut. For more information, visit www.stable-management.com.

Paula Ryan lives in Kansas City, Missouri, with her husband, son, and numerous pets. She has loved both writing and horses since childhood and shows no sign of getting over either of them any time soon. You can email Paula at crowshaven@sbcglobal.net.

Patti Schonlau

Terri Smith is a lifelong rider who lives in the suburbs southwest of Houston and works as a technical writer for the oil and gas industry. You can e-mail Terri at terrismith@tech-editor.com.

Melinda Stiles writes and rides in Idaho with the majesty of nature as backdrop and inspiration for both. She has been published in newspapers, magazines, and anthologies. She is currently enjoying compiling a collection of essays. She can be reached at stilesms@live.com.

Ann Louise Truschel has been a medical and business writer for more than three decades. She prepares drug and device submissions to the U.S. Food and Drug Administration for pharmaceutical companies; ghosts monographs, journal articles, and books for physicians; writes consumer health articles for newspapers, magazines, and newsletters; and prepares technology assessments for the Department of Defense. Visit her at www.desertwriter.com.

Ellen Nicholson Walker is a teacher, writer, and horseman. She is a volunteer instructor for 4-H and has been riding and taking care of horses for more than forty years. Currently, she is busy working on two young adult novels and a picture book that all involve horses, and playing with two Hungarian horses and a Welsh pony.

Jennifer Walker is a lifelong lover of Arabian horses and a lifelong hater of falling off of them. When she's not stuck in an office writing business reports, she writes articles about life with horses (and anything else that comes to mind) and currently has several books in various stages of completion. She is attempting to survive dressage training and hopes to some day make it out of training level.

Samantha Ducloux Waltz is an award-winning freelance writer in Portland, Oregon.

Her essays can be seen in the Chicken Soup for the Soul series, a Cup of Comfort series, and a number of magazines. She has also published fiction and nonfiction under the names Samantha Ducloux and Samellyn Wood.

Harry Werner, D.V.M., has practiced equine medicine and surgery since his 1974 graduation from the University of Pennsylvania School of Veterinary Medicine. He has operated a general equine practice in northern Connecticut since 1979. The primarily ambulatory practice has a clinic that handles emergency care, internal medicine cases, and minor surgery. Dr. Werner's special interests include lameness, prepurchase examinations, wellness care, and owner education. Dr. Werner is the 2008 president-elect of the American Association of Equine Practitioners (AAEP). He has held positions as AAEP treasurer, chair of the AAEP Purchase Examination Committee, and president of the Connecticut Veterinary Medical Association. He has made presentations at AAEP conventions on lameness in sport horses and prepurchase examinations, and served on numerous panels including lameness in sport horses and Lyme disease. He has coauthored publications on equine Lyme disease and prepurchase examination guidelines and writes frequently for industry publications.

Angelina Wilson is a professional journalist whose articles have appeared in publications ranging from the *Parkersburg News* to *Bird Watcher's Digest*. She graduated from Ohio University, where she majored in magazine journalism and showed with the intercollegiate equestrian team in the walk/trot division. She enjoys spending her free time riding her thoroughbreds, Murphy and Chrome, as well as traveling to watch show-jumping competitions.

Diane Wilson has been in love with horses since the age of three when she was soundly kicked in the shin by a carnival pony visiting her Illinois hometown. Now living in California, she writes young adult novels that always feature a horse.

Vanessa Wright is the author of more than 300 works of fiction and nonfiction published through organizations including K12, Inc. and National Endowment for the Humanities EDSITEment. She is also a riding instructor, certified by the American Riding Instructors Association, and an equine photographer whose work has been featured in promotional and educational materials for equine nonprofits and showcased in galleries nationwide.

The Photographers

Sarah K. Andrew is one of the most exciting and talented young equine photographers to debut in years. In the last few years, Sarah and her camera have become well-known at New York and New Jersey racetracks and other equine sport venues. Her work has been featured in many publications, including the *New York Times*, and hangs proudly on many a horse owner's wall. For more information, visit her at www.rockandracehorses.com.

Jim Arnold is a leading Texas-based equine photographer. As a horse owner and lover, he prides himself in being able to capture horses at the peak of their performance, revealing their personalities and athletic skills. Jim's work appears in numerous equestrian publications, including *Quarter Horse News* and the *Cutting Horse Chatter*. For the last seven years he has been focusing on Texas Fasig-Tipton sales for *Blood-Horse*, *Thoroughbred Times*, and the *Texas Thoroughbred*. His portraits include some of the leading sires of thoroughbred racing at their home farms. Visit Jim's website at www.jarnoldphoto.com.

Amanda Borozinski is a full-time reporter and photographer for the *Keene Sentinel*, a daily newspaper in Keene, New Hampshire. Her work has appeared in *Guideposts* magazine, *Positive Thinking* magazine, the *Northern New England Review*, the *Oklahoma Review*, the *Boston Globe* and TheHorse.com. In 2008, she was awarded a fellowship from the prestigious MacDowell Colony and spent three secluded weeks working on an upcoming book project. Amanda can be reached at aboro@ptcnh.net.

Sharon P. Fibelkorn is a freelance photojournalist known for her keen eye and refined editorial work, specializing in action photography. As a working photographer, her pictures have added visual illustration to most of the top publications throughout the world both as editorial and advertising. But it's those intimate portraits that grace personal homes and barns that have a special place in her soul. To simply say she enjoys taking a picture isn't enough. To say she has enjoyed her journey in life while creating and living moments with her subjects would be a better statement.

Susan Friedman is an award-winning documentary filmmaker and photographer with twenty-four years of experience in the field of education. She is currently on the faculty at the University of California, Santa Cruz. Susan has been a still photographer for many years and has had one-women shows both nationally and internationally. Her book of documentary photographs for the Sierra Club, *A Separate Place*, was published in 1974 and her work is collected in the Museum of Modern Art in New York, the Oakland Museum, and the Bibliothèque National in Paris. Visit Susan at www.susanfriedmanphoto.com or email her at whatisup@earthlink.net.

Morgan Ong is the director of photography for Petconnection.com. Formerly the deputy director of photography for Knight Ridder/Tribune News Service in Washington, DC, Morgan also served as photo editor in the Washington bureau of the Associated Press.

Theresa Peluso volunteers at Horses and the Handicapped, a North American Riding for the Handicapped Association (NARHA) premiere accredited facility that provides equine-assisted activities and hippotherapy for physically, emotionally, and cognitively challenged students from ages four to seventy-four on a scholarship basis. Theresa is the coauthor of the bestselling *Chicken Soup for the Horse Lover's Soul*, its sequel, *Chicken Soup for the Horse Lover's Soul II*, and several other titles in the Chicken Soup for the Soul series. Her photographs featured here are of the equine partners who are an integral part of the program's success. For more information, visit www.handhmagic.org and NARHA at www.narha.org.

Norman L. Rehme holds the degrees of master of photography and photographic craftsman. He photographs a wide variety of subjects from infants to the elderly and landscapes to animals. Some of the most popular models for him now are his grandchildren. Norman collaborates with his author wife, Carol. The horses in this publication were captured on a Canon 1Ds Mark III with a 600 millimeter lens. "I enjoyed the evening light as it shone peacefully upon these grazing horses," Norman says. Visit him at www.rehme.com.

Kristen Reiter, D.V.M., is an award-winning equine photographer whose works have graced the pages of multiple books and nationally distributed equestrian magazines. In addition, her photographs have routinely been utilized by the Appaloosa Horse Club for advertising and promotion.

Shane Salley lives in Allen, Texas, and works for parks and recreation. He enjoys photography, cycling, and working out.

Troy Snow is a professional freelance photographer whose work has been widely appreciated and published. Along with a team from Best Friends Animal Society, he went to the Gulf Coast in the aftermath of Hurricane Katrina to help animals and people. The stories from that rescue effort are told in his stunning pictures in *Not Left Behind: Rescuing the Pets of New Orleans* (Yorkville Press). Troy's pictures can be found on the Best Friends website at www.bestfriends.org and at www.troysnowphoto.com.

Sara Stafford has been a horse lover all her life and a rider since she was ten. Taking pictures is her other passion and she hopes to start a business in equine photography. Sara finds inspiration and willing subjects for her photos while working at one of the largest Lipizzan breeding farms in the country, White Horse Vale, in Goldendale, Washington.

Vanessa Wright is the author of more than 300 works of fiction and nonfiction published through organizations including K12, Inc. and the National Endowment for the Humanities EDSITEment. She is also a riding instructor, certified by the American Riding Instructors Association, and an equine photographer whose work has been featured in promotional and educational materials for equine nonprofits and showcased in galleries across New England.

The Authors

Marty Becker, D.V.M., is the regularly featured veterinarian on ABC-TV's *Good Morning America*, a frequent veterinary contributor to *The Martha Stewart Show*, and the host of the PBS series *The Pet Doctor with Marty Becker*, which airs in hundreds of markets nationwide. In his multifaceted twenty-eight year career, Dr. Becker has been at the forefront of changing the way we interact with and take responsibility for our pets. He is the author of the bestselling book, *Becoming Your Dog's Best Friend*, and the coauthor of the *New York Times* bestseller *Chicken Soup for the Cat Lover's Soul* as well as a pet-care feature for newspapers across America and Canada syndicated through Universal Press. Often called "America's veterinarian," he has been named Companion Animal Veterinarian of the Year by the Delta Society and the American Veterinary Medical Association.

Gina Spadafori is the author of an award-winning weekly column on pets and their care, which is syndicated throughout North America and Canada by Universal Press. She is a bestselling author of several pet books, which have sold 375,000 copies combined, including *Why Do Cats Always Land on Their Feet?* and *Cats for Dummies*. Along with coauthor Dr. Paul D. Pion, she received the Cat Writers' Association awards for the best work on feline nutrition, best work on feline behavior, and best work on responsible cat care for *Cats for Dummies*. She has served on the board of directors for both the Cat Writers' Association, Inc. and the Dog Writers Association of America.

Audrey Pavia is a former editor of *Horse Illustrated* magazine and an award-winning freelance writer specializing in equine subjects. She is the author of several horse books, including *Horses for Dummies*, *Horseback Riding for Dummies*, and *Trail Riding: A Complete Guide*. She has authored hundreds of articles on equine topics in a number of horse publications, including *Western Horseman*, *The Trail Rider*, *Equestrian Retailer*, *Horses USA*, *Appaloosa Journal*, *Paint Horse Journal*, *Quarter Horses USA*, *Equine Veterinary Management*, and *USDF Connection* magazines.

Mikkel Becker is an intercultural communications major from Washington State University. She has been active in the quarter horse show circuit and is a three-time Canadian National Champion in Western Pleasure and Hunter Under Saddle. Mikkel is a contributing author to Knight Ridder newspapers, *Cat Fancy* magazine, and *Chicken Soup for the Horse Lover's Soul*.

Copyright Credits

(continued from page ii)

Index